Manche

Manchester

Thom Cuell

Dostoyevsky Wannabe Cities
An Imprint of Dostoyevsky Wannabe

First Published in 2018
by Dostoyevsky Wannabe Cities
All rights reserved
© All copyright reverts to individual authors

Dostoyevsky Wannabe Cities is an imprint of Dostoyevsky Wannabe publishing.

This anthology is a work of fiction. The names, characters and incidents portrayed in it are the work of the author's imagination. Any resemblance to actual persons, living or dead, events or localities is entirely coincidental.

Cover Design by Dostoyevsky Wannabe Design
dostoyevskywannabe.com

ISBN-978-1723215674
ISBN-1723215678

No parts of this publication may be reproduced, stored in a retrieval system, or transmitted in any form or by any means, electronic, mechanical, photocopying, recording, or otherwise, without the prior written permission of the copyright owner.

This book is sold subject to the condition that it shall not, by way of trade or otherwise, be lent, resold, hired out, or otherwise circulated without the publisher's prior consent in any form of binding or cover other than that in which it is published and without a similar condition including this condition being imposed on the subsequent purchaser. Under no circumstances may any part of this book be photocopied for resale.

Acknowledgments

Thanks first of all must go to Thom Cuell who agreed to guest-edit this *Dostoyevsky Wannabe Cities: Manchester* anthology and to bring in so many great contributors. Also thanks to Sarah-Clare Conlon for her write up of the book and of the event that is connected to the book on the Creative Tourist site.

By the time you read this we'll know if anyone bothered to come along to the event, the aim was to unite independently minded people of Manchester with Manchester's independent presses and so we hope a few people turn up to buy the wares on offer. Neither of us are employed by or funded to do Dostoyevsky Wannabe in any way and we spend infinitely more time typesetting and designing covers for books than we do getting out and about to all of the many independent literary and artistic things that go on in Manchester so, for us, whether people turn up to the event at Plant Noma at the end of July or not, it'll be cool to meet the writers who have contributed to this volume and also to meet the presses and art collectives who have agreed to be involved in our 'book fair thing' more widely: zimZalla, if p then q, Knives, Forks & Spoons, Generic Greeting and Dodo Ink.

A short note on Lee Rourke. Lee was billed as being in this anthology and he was writing a story especially for it. Unfortunately due to the speedy turnaround of this project, the story wasn't quite ready and we had to go to print without him. Happily, we have been able to arrange for Minor Literature[s] to agree to put his story out when it is ready by way of an online extension of this book.

Finally, thanks to Jess, Joe and Ben and Plant Noma for creating such an strangely flexible (and free) space and to Ailsa from Living Room Dance Club for almost DJing until we re-orientated the event to become more of a sober(-ish) Saturday afternoon book fair than a full on rave.

—Dostoyevsky Wannabe Editors, Summer 2018

CONTENTS

Tristan Burke	9
Sian Cummins	17
Peter Wild	31
Sarah-Clare Conlon	43
Anthony Trevelyan	51
Bryony Bates	65
Valerie O'Riordan	73
Thom Cuell	91
Contributors	103

Tristan Burke

Tristan Burke

Anecdotes

On Fridays in winter, the Jewish lads of North Manchester Grammar School for Boys would be allowed to leave early, to reach home before sundown. In the light of the Shabbat candles, the soot from Manchester's chimneys would show as a thin line of black where their shirt collars protruded above their blazers. The Shudehill Food Fight of 1757 was not as fun as it sounds; rioting broke out from anger directed towards the rapidly developing capitalist class who controlled the food supply. Outside a house in the redbrick suburbs, two housewives had hung their washing out. A man walking past said to one of them that he could see which of the two neighbours used Persil. Thomas Percival was a linen weaver in Levenshulme who believed in universal liberty. When Lord Strange brought his men into Manchester to seize the city's munitions, he died in a street skirmish, as can be read about in *The beginning of Civil Warres in England, or Terrible News from the North*. The last execution in England took place at Strangeways. On his last night the condemned man dreamt that the rope would break three times. A man in the Printworks had a party trick. He would plunge his hand into a bucket of molten lead and remove it unscathed. When an apprentice attempted the same feat, he lost his hand. A criminal fled up the big wheel in Piccadilly Gardens. Once the gardens represented freedom even in their orderly planting, now they are set out as a failed architecture of control. A man ate an apple only because he was a mathematician. A neighbour's daughter with a flair for chemistry made a bomb and set it off on the back field, another son played with his father's service revolver. In St Mary's Church on Mulberry Street a woman prays before each station of the cross. In the Town Hall, between the marble statues of councillors and MPs, staff sometimes catch sight of the ghost of a Victorian policeman, truncheon ready in hand. When the candidates for the BNP knocked in error at a British Indian family's door they did

Manchester

not know what to say to them. The destitute take spice become like statues beneath the beshitten and besmeared Victoriana that clutters the streets. There was a man down the road who remembered the Boer Wars. He gave a local boy a set of annuals, *Boys' Own* adventure periodicals, which gathered dust and decayed beneath his bed. When Thomas de Quincey lay on his sofa in Grasmere in his opium deliria, he saw Manchester as it is today, a towering prison of grey fire from a Piranesi print. That was how the Irish labourer saw it when he arrived in 1834. That was how my mother saw it when she arrived in 1975 on her first trip North. The names of the Peterloo dead are: John Ashton, John Ashworth, William Bradshaw, Thomas Buckley, Robert Campbell, James Crompton, Edmund Dawson, William Dawson, Margaret Downes, William Evans, William Fildes, Mary Heys, Sarah Jones, John Lees, Arthur Neil, Martha Partington, John Rhodes, Joshua Whitworth. William Fildes was two years old. Down with 'em! Chop 'em down my brave boys: give them no quarter they want to take our Beef & Pudding from us! ---- & remember the more you kill the less poor rates you'll have to pay so go at it Lads show your courage & your Loyalty!

Tristan Burke

The three disciplinary centres of proud Victorian Manchester were designed by Alfred Waterhouse: Strangeways Prison, the Town Hall, the Manchester Museum. One was for the classification of correct knowledge, one for the administration of urban space and activity, one for the production of docile subjects. Which one is which? From Oxford Road one cannot see Strangeways but we all know the tower is looming just over the horizon. Who is it fooling that its tower is for ventilation? Its panoptic vision still dominates the city. For the administration of urban space and time, for the classification of correct knowledge, for the production of docile subjects. Its tower makes claims to a centre. The meeting place of long straight roads, lest the mill owners, who in their carriages with assurance sit, must see the human refuse they left behind: Bury New Road, Cheetham Hill Road, Rochdale Road, Oldham Road, Bradford Road, Ashton Old Road, Hyde Road, Stockport Road, Anson Road, Oxford Road, Princess Road, Chester Road, Regent Road. One does not walk through Manchester as much as travel to and from it, through its poverty and its leafy suburbs, both of which are screened by the edges of its conduits in and out. It does not have the urban density of old cities. It is abstract, premeditated, and cruel. A walk through Manchester would take us, only, between its three disciplinary centres, where we might glimpse, as at the edge of a photograph, attempts to carve out a more liveable life or a space of potentiality under the shadow of its all-seeing ventilation tower. Or perhaps, in the suburbs, arranged too like a panopticon, a minor life may emerge. Thus a prisoner emerges from the gates of Strangeways with a mind to look into the eyes of a mummy, a stuffed orangutan or a Roman coin. Down Bury New Road and Great Ducie Street, the A56, past a fancy dress warehouse where, perhaps, he can change his clothes, buy a parka, a business suit, get that haircut that is still in fashion. Past another panopticon, named for another panopticon, the MEN, past Cheetham's Library and the ghost of Marx where knowledge was not classified, but merely, gently locked up. Left off Victoria

Manchester

Street, through Cathedral Gardens where there is a homeless man to smile at in the cold mornings and then forget how he looks, under the transparency of Urbis. Past where the bomb was, past where the bomb was, past where they printed newspapers. Along Corporation Street, which holds the Cotton Exchange, with its circular glass capsule where spectator and observer are reversed, Cross Street Chapel, over the bones of the plague. Little bits of Utopia capping death and Ship Canal House which dreamt of moving the seas like Moses with an army of Irish navvies. And the Town Hall. From there down Mount Street, on the one hand the Quaker Meeting House, square, against the Central Library, circular. The Quaker square creates a circle, at corners there is openness. The library is a perimeter, a hemming in with coats of arms and great writers on illuminated stained glass windows (an illuminated Shakespeare would leave no space for negative capability), a proper place for the circulation of knowledge, a strict space for observation. And onto another of those roads that striates the city. Oxford Road begins with a whited sepulchre, St Peter's Square, where the memories of a massacre are entombed by a pristine war memorial, a pristine tram stop, a pristine fountain, pristine flowerbeds (low maintenance shrubs), pristine glass offices, palaces waiting for the soldiers' blood and sighs. So far, our prisoner's journey has taken us, not down the expressways for the bourgeoisie but through the central zone, the safe zone, the business zone, where the wretched might blot the margins but do not threaten the carefully constructed order of the city, for the ventilation towers loom over them as an ever present reminder. This zone has been consolidated in recent years, and around the endless canyon of Oxford Road clustered the very existence the road should veil, interlaced with the evidence of its masters, those Victorian and Edwardian officers that so proudly proclaimed the names of their companies, for they dreamt they would always be there, these globalisers who never imagined that the centres of their own capitalist dominance would shift globally, and who zombielike return to the scenes of their deaths, Refuge

Assurance, KPMG. And what of what was lost? The Peace Gardens where the war memorial now stands; a symbolically redundant plaque to the nuclear free city; the ghost of the basement of the Dutch Pancake House, its enormous plates telling the history of early capitalism, its fliptop bottles of Grolsch; the ghost of the Cornerhouse and of Alan Turing's cruising spot outside the Salisbury, both already revenantial under the railway's wrecking ball, these haunts haunting under the exorcism of infrastructural organisation. And over the old BBC, Circle Square, can only half hide its own panoptic dreams under the playful demicancellation of its advertising copy. A spectre is haunting Manchester, the spectre of control. Past fences to keep the homeless out, and shipping containers to keep the students in, past the best falafel in the city, looms the Byzantine edifice of the university. Here George Gissing, who knew of all cities' lower depths, of their hellish degradation and their divisions of power was expelled for stealing from the treasury to rescue a prostitute and remains unspoken of in the list of famous alumni. Under an arch, a spider crab keeps guard, many armed, and across the road another cylinder looms, a tin of baked beans, a friendly parody, for whose half smiling face every point is visible.

Sian Cummins

Sian Cummins

Three Modern Dramatists

This is a story about loneliness, but it has a happy ending.

She is a woman in pain; not all the time. Sometimes. It catches her by surprise. Frilled and scalloped in places inside, tightened harshly where torn. Tough – she's decided she's tougher now, because weathered by rough emergency. But all of that is for another story.

It is 9th August 2017 and she's decided to have another look for That Book. She's feeling pissed off about the TV and wondering if she is setting herself up here for more disappointment. It's bound to be gone. Old books are weeded out she's fairly sure; especially those with huge amounts of wilful damage, and it's been 20 years. But how amazing would it be to see it again.

She's still surprised at how unchanged the library is. Oh, don't get us wrong. It's been modernised and brightened, whole floors of the dry old catalogue decks razed and the pouffes and chaises in primary colours rolled in. Perspex between workstations.

She has stood on Oxford Road and felt the past and future rip through her like light ribbons in time lapse photography. Things change and they never change on that clogged ley line of the gentrifying and crumbled. She looks at the ridiculous height of the Holy Name Church and the sawn-off steps of the Steve Biko Building where student bums will sit no more, and she feels erased, rubbed out, and commemorated forever. Still – what – young? – and here she is again.

Whole floors of the library given a makeover, but not Blue 3. The Perspex dividers are there but the layout and fabric are mostly untouched. It smells the same. There must be a cell or two of her teenage skin still circulating in the dust. Typed slips at the end of rows read 'Caution: kicksteps in aisles' and some of those have simply been painted over as the synonymous blue has been re-lashed over the years. A corner is peeling up and she sees an older and different shade of blue, and nostalgia stabs her.

Manchester

It must surely be gone. Sensible logic says so. Librarians may have more of a sense of humour than most, but destruction and vandalism are what they are. A library is an official structure, if a liberal one; webbed up in cataloguing and customer interface and accountability. And the book was middle-aged already in 1997, a seventies edition. She has seen in her local library - books barely ten years old on sale in the 10p racks, some with a little rip or a missing page, some with nothing wrong at all. They're ruthless. So That Book would have to have kept its head down to survive. Seriously. It will be a miracle if it's still there.

She's working her way towards the right classification. She doesn't even remember what the book is called. Believe us if you can, the book wasn't her first thought on returning to the city. For a couple of years she's relentlessly haunted the places where nostalgia gallops down the street at the pace of a bleeding nose and she's never thought of it - not once, not ever. She's even spent time in the library without considering that it's up there somewhere, maybe, perhaps. Her wishes are with other ghosts. And then a week ago she went up to Blue 3 and pulled a pile of the plays out in a rush, five minutes before the end of lunch. It wasn't there.

Today she drifts her hand along the end of the work benches. It's summer-quiet and she flicks up the front covers of some of the books abandoned in piles against the desk dividers, keeping the shelving staff in ear buds and rent. Many have been re-covered in matte hardback, red, blue, manila, with gold letters embossed along the spines. The original covers flap stiffly inside. It makes browsing mundane, more thrilling, and difficult. One re-covered book is more battered than the ones around it, and yet someone has been here, in the summer holidays, finding it useful. The hardback shell is hanging by a few threads and when she lifts it gently she sees a mawkish-faced sun rising above a knotted snake. *Arduus ad solem*, striving towards the sun, the old university crest. A crusty old survivor from the pre-rebrand days. There is hope.

She has tried, now and again in the intervening years, to

track down the artist. Someone must have been as impressed by the book as she has been. She's always felt that. It was in a large university library in a section serving a very oversubscribed department - (she accepts and understands her own mediocrity) – and so must have passed through many hands. How is it not a legend of the university, like the secret floor at the top of Stopford, or the ghost of Owens Park Tower? She also knows and accepts that she never was one of the cool kids at the centre of it all. If there is a community of in-the-know around the book she is excluded from it. She's lost contact with students from her own course, having preferred the company of the more straightforward archaeology kids. If anyone does remember it from the English lot, she can't ask them. Over the years, she has used Google a few times to enter long inept descriptions of it. It didn't show up. In a way, she was relieved. She still wonders sometimes who drew the pictures where they shouldn't have.

When Facebook came around she posted a couple of things on groups that concerned themselves with the city and the university. She went into quite a lot of detail and got a couple of likes but no follow-through. She even tagged some of the people: why did you like this post; do you know more? Then she forgot for a while about the artist and their strange graffiti – you should not get the impression that she thought about the book continuously for all those years. In time, Facebook became a sort of dazed academic symposium where nothing much was being said beyond insults and demands for evidence.

She first finds the book in 1997. She is a girl in pain, with blood caked inside her nose and her right big toenail black and loose inside her Gazelles. But all that's for another story. A girl? At 19, a 'woman', if she were to be abducted or pushed in the canal. But whatever the papers might call her in their hypothetical murder ballad, to herself she is a 'girl'.

Her timetable for the final year is a potch of stuff that might help her nebulous career ambitions, and stuff she put down in a rush and is stuck with. This unit is in the second category: 'Three modern dramatists: Beckett, Orton and Pinter'. Filler. Ballast. Beans on toast.

There is an envelope of photocopies stapled to the back of her list of allocations. She stuffs this into her bag and the staple comes out on the way home. In no order, she reads some of the photocopied extracts. She slides to the floor, back to her white chipboard wardrobe, and doesn't move for over an hour. The first one. The writer swears, uses words like she hears every day, and others – posher – in phrases are as quotable as a pop song. She laughs out loud at some bits. She doesn't remember laughing like this, except at high school at their gawking group obsessions – magazines and sketch shows – until her cheekbones ached. As a student, laughter is rationed. But no one else is at home, and this writing… It's sort of high-polished, sneery, like lots of people here try to be, but with the nastiness redirected somehow.

In a different extract on another sheet, ordinary things are made scarier than infinity. This writer leans heavily on the everyday until you're forced head first through the normal and out the other side into uncanny. This one makes her laugh, too. It makes her look around the grotty room, with lipstick on the mirror and a dirty plate on the floor and think – I see this. I can't change it, but I see it. Then she puts the photocopies back in the bag and forgets them until the summer is almost over.

Before the start of term she tries to do the research she should have done before selecting the course unit. She grabs a few books from the reading list. Sharp black and white photos of a sharp man in the sort of glasses you just don't see anymore. Then, a young one in jeans and a t-shirt. Chubby face, smirking. She flips the book over to the blurb. Joe Orton. Celebrated playwright for just three years before his violent death at the age of 34. Violent death? Fuck, really? She thinks – car crash? She skims the inside for clues. She finds: murder. A writer, only a writer, brought as photocopied sheets to a classroom; murdered in her parents' lifetime. Not in a dirty Elizabethan tavern. Recent. Shit. Joe

Orton. Joe. Battered to death by his boyfriend. Poor Joe.

She spends the last week of summer seeking out doomed Joe. She reads some of his stuff and matches him to the pop-song phrasing that made her laugh in her horrible flat. She reads everything she can find by him and everything she can find about him. The six-month prison sentence for cutting and pasting library books makes her laugh again. Here's someone who lived fast and took the piss wherever it was found. She's listened well to the lectures on cultural materialism and knows that any artist's work is part of their physical world and the bruises it leaves on them. This is not a difficult concept for an NME-reading teenager who knows what every band member had for breakfast and whether it's codified in the songs. She reads the diaries and sometimes he seems arch and snippy – and, you'd have hated me, she thinks – but then she reads something else about how warm he was. Likeable and rebellious and suddenly destroyed. The first scene of the biography, the murder scene in savage detail, stays with her forever and becomes an archetype for her understanding of pity and pain.

In September, aching with infatuation, she makes her way to the first class. The lecturer affects a Trotsky beard and a withered tank top. He is plummy, with Oxford credentials, but also a giant inverted snob. They start with a TV script by Joe about a holiday camp. The lecturer is keen to get it over with quickly. He says in his opening gloss that 'Orton is by far the weaker of the three'. Then he informs the class that 'none of you lot will have been to a holiday camp.' Meaning, because they are 'too' 'middle class'. He is crass and openly hostile about and towards the adult people he is paid to teach, while wearing the optional arrogance of the career academic.

She never knows how to address these teachers. You don't say 'Dr' anything, unless you want to be laughed at. She doesn't feel on first-name terms with this fat old snoot. She finds she is putting her hand up in the air. God. But what the hell.

'I actually have been to Butlins,' she tells him and the

class. 'I get the full grant, too. Anyway, I've seen first-hand what the play is getting at. These people are control freaks. I mean you see it everywhere, don't you? Dress codes in clubs? Fun is regimented. Always has been.' She puts her hand down.

'There's always one,' sighs the tutor. 'Wants to prove there's dirt under their fingernails.' He ignores the rest of what she says.

She is a raw nerve and has been since registration week. She expected social and personal nirvana, but the reality has been more solitary, administrative and neutral. But her excitement remains: unbottled. She fizzes. She never does it, but she does imagine this – tearing herself with her own blunt fingernails. (Real dirt and all). Drawing the map from fear to exhilaration, self-disgust to self-obsession and back, in meat-pink lines. She does this – picks constellations of tiny blocked pores on her inner thighs. They scar white. Destruction isn't creation, it's interpretation. Only a state change, but still a homage.

And so, they're covering Beckett next but now she wants to know more about Pinter. You know: she senses darkness skin's thickness away but she doesn't turn to look at it. She distracts herself with tiny fetishes and compulsions, for many years. When she is finally propelled into a living nightmare…but more of that later. Perhaps. Pinter, on the other hand, sees the dark everywhere and beckons it out – from under the chairs, lurking in the nozzle of the hoover. She piles the editions of his plays on top of Beckett. In 1997, Pinter is alive. This is its own thrill. This degree course is very uncomfortable with the modern age. They've frolicked for months in knights and faeries and English that is barely English and now here's a man of flesh who lives in London – AND – was a friend of Joe.

She looks along the anonymised red linen spines of the criticism works. Harold Pinter. Gold embossed. She takes one down at random. We swear, at random. She adds it to her pile, she checks it out with the others and she takes it home.

Pinter is the writer of the ordinary scenes that go slowly mad. A fingernail grazing a palm with all the weight of the universe. She believes him to be blunt, forbidding and infectiously menacing. Clever, an actor, the man with the sort of glasses you don't see any more. He has written essays on Nicaragua. His political anger is completely addictive. She doesn't skim the red book because she doesn't want to miss anything.

She is reading late into the night when she turns over and sees that the facing page is different to the others. The writing is off at a slant but the text carries on uninterrupted. It's photocopied, she realises. The paper is lower quality, harsh white. She turns it.

There is a little clump of the bright white photocopied pages, at the centre of the book. Someone has gone to the effort of removing the pages so that the rest of the book isn't torn, photocopying them, cutting them to size and stitching them back into the book somehow. It's an intricate job. By rights, the whole book should be falling apart but she might not have noticed the thin line of sharp white running around its middle if she hadn't been reading it so closely. When the mystery saboteur put them back in, they did it so that every other double-page spread was blank.

On the first new blank spread, the artist/vandal has drawn two cartoons. They are simple characters, with long noses, receding chins and sad little overbites. On the left-hand page, the cartoon is captioned ASTON FIXES THE PLUG in neat block caps and is a line drawing of the character sitting on a realistically saggy mattress, fixing a plug. It's a scene from *The Caretaker*. On the facing page, there is another cartoon from the same play, captioned MICK SHOWS DAVIES THE HOOVER. In the cartoon, terrified Davies kneels with shock lines coming out of his head, his three-fingered hands pleading with Mick to stop. Mick bends over Davies, bearing down on him with the nozzle and an accusing finger, big dot-and-line eyes, long nose and overbite expressing wild fury.

The following spread is blank, but for these handwritten

lines at the top left of the first page:

These pages are a commentary on the female characters in The Caretaker.

That almost knocks her flat. She turns over:

These two pages are about Pinter's use of silence in his plays.

And on the next spread:

These two pages are about Catholics and sex.

Then:

My mother always told me to use a condom, which is a bit ridiculous because she's past the menopause and there's no chance of her getting pregnant.

Finally, in different handwriting on the final blank spread:

This is where the funny bloke ran out of funny things to say.

It sits in her hand and smells of dust and libraries and is real. She loves it. Maybe it's the sort of knowing intertextual joke that's run of the mill in public school, but to her it's daring. She feels there is real affection for Pinter in it; for his characters, even for the defaced critique, and the implicit link to Joe Orton, another defacer of library books. The artist has drawn a line between them all on purpose, including herself, the anticipated, unwitting reader. The person who did it leans into the future and laughs with her. Even if it is a public-school joke and they were aiming at someone who was bottle-fed Pinter, they wouldn't have begrudged her a giggle. She loves it. She wants it. It seems almost right to steal it, and she has done worse. Stealing it would mean returning it to the library and checking it back in, then hiding in a corner and picking out the magnetic strip. Then out, with it tucked at the bottom of her bag to live with her forever.

But. What would be its life? She is prescient now, as she sees its fate would be to crawl between a series of woodchipped rooms, warped and squashed among other, lesser books in a DelMonte box. She won't let anyone else touch it, she will look at it rarely, and it will end its life in shreds when she accidentally takes it out at a messy party. The artist doesn't see her. She has felt for a moment that she was holding hands across time with the unknown artist, with the Pinter critic, with Pinter, and even with Joe, but that chain is broken by herself – the weak and anonymous link. No more than a reader among more. She is suddenly angry and wants it gone. It belongs in the halogen dim of the library where another unsuspecting young browser can be illuminated, entertained and, finally, disillusioned by it. She takes it back that same night, queueing for a bus in the rain.

Two years later, in 1999, she moves to London.

She is there for years. She likes to tell people that those are her 'wilderness years' but in fact plenty does happen. She is close to, but unscathed by, a catastrophe. She changes career three times. She loves and loses and then again, and again.

In 2002 she happens to be in Islington, buys a pocket A to Z and finds Noel Road. She stands outside number 25 and is irritated by the green plaque. She feels it isn't fair on the current occupants, should they not know what went on at their smart address, beyond 'John Kingsley Orton… lived here.' Besides, it should be blue.

In 2006 she sees Harold Pinter read, the only time she ever does, and falls in love all over again with his conviction in the face of the darkness he most certainly does face. In response to a question he as good as insists that he will not live to write another play.

She remembers the book a few times and talks to people about it a few times. Some think it's interesting, even want to talk back to her about it. At one party she is a bit too high and excited and is pulled up by a Shoreditch alpha female over her Joe crush: 'I mean, you don't really like the plays do you? It's just that he's forever young. You don't see anyone mooning over black and white photos of Alan Ayckbourn, do you? You're having your Candle in the Wind moment, aren't you, sweetheart?' What is most refreshing about this encounter is that she instantly senses – no, knows – that this woman is wrong on almost every count.

In 2008, Christmas, she is sitting in a stuffed front room,

arm-of-chair seating room only, a plate of buffet on one knee and one of the new generation of babies on the other. Her phone makes a noise and she roots for it and finds out that Harold Pinter is dead.

It's soon after that she makes her first, quickly abandoned attempts to hunt out the book and its saboteur online.

In 2010 she manages to enjoy *Waiting for Godot*, finally suppressing the echo of the Three Modern Dramatists lecturer who went on, and on, and on about Beckett. Silence, after all.

In time, she returns to Manchester. Her child is born there and on this day in August 2017 waits, healthy and cheerful, to be picked up from a sweet day nursery. But finally, too, things have happened and she has been made to look straight into the darkness. Wade in to it - and it sticks to her like tar.

She is hot, which makes things pull and tighten, and she is pissed off with TV and the internet. There seems to be insufficient Joe. With no disrespect to the other famous death about to celebrate a decades-long anniversary, there is more than enough August 2017 for both of them.

It is still there.

Today she has more time. She flicks through quite a few books before finding the almost invisible strip of white through one of the works of criticism lined up in their uniform red jackets. She says something like 'shit!' out loud and then looks around, but it's summer and there's no one else here. She gently turns to the white centre, expecting, maybe, deterioration. There is none. There are the cartoons, the jokes; not replaced or fixed or binned. Possibly nobody cares enough to rectify the vandalism. Possibly librarians' sense of humour rebels in hiding. Possibly she is the only person who has ever found the hidden centre of the book, or one in very few. She supposes that's possible, even over 20 years.

This was a story about loneliness and it still is. But. Her hand covers the same warm red linen and paper as that of her teenage self. People out there in the sun, on the grass, are oblivious. She feels tougher these days, but she also feels gentler. She brings another new layer of herself to the book, the writing she came to love as an unhappy student, and her returns to it over time – and it is the understanding that all these things matter. It is still unsatisfactory, she supposes, to be only a reader. But she gets the joke when some wouldn't, and that means the book is for her. She remembered it, it was here when she came to look, and that also means it is for her.

She could steal it. She has certainly done worse. She could look again for the artist, but really she doesn't need to. They have found her.

She takes some photos, which feels like another kind of theft, kisses the book, and replaces it.

Peter Wild

Nico and the Boys

"Today," Bobby said, his face inches from my own. "Today is the day."

He was hunched over me. I was in my sleeping bag. I'd been sleeping. I was groggy. "Today is what?" I said.

He held up what I thought was a blade.

"Today," he said, brandishing.

It wasn't a blade. It was a letter opener.

"Is that a letter opener?" I asked him.

"It doesn't matter what it is. It'll do," he answered me.

"It'll do for what?"

"For what we need."

It was me and Bobby Zero. We were young. We were kings. We were captains. If you asked us, we'd tell you we'd sprung whole from the skull of Athena. I got that from Bobby, didn't know what it meant but liked it an awful lot, to the extent that I'd say it sometimes when I was on my own, maybe last thing at night, in bed in the dark. The words were a kind of music. They were the soundtrack to our days which stretched before us uninterrupted and without end for it was the summer. The summer of the second year I had been without a person to call my own, without a family, without a home, without root or branch. I lived in a factory. Or rather I lived in a partial factory. I don't know if builders had started work and stopped or if builders had completed work and then circumstance had prevailed against them but it was a neither one thing or another kind of place. Scaffolding, concrete walls that feebly extended skyward, jutting sideways rocks where other floors might have been or were planned for, dirty windows with wiry metal grates, hard metal spikes poking out like startled fingers. There was a cellar area that was covered to the elements. I'd chanced upon a discarded Calor gas cooker. I stole bedding from a washing line, half-inched a stanky sleeping bag. Bobby kept me fed and watered most days. It wasn't always easy to be clean but I did my best. I got by. There was the age difference, of course, but Bobby said he was the Hotspur to my Falstaff.

Manchester

Over my head but again I appreciated the music.

"Eh?" Bobby said, showing me first one side and then the other of his makeshift weapon.

"Where ja find that?"

"Neither here nor there, compadre."

I nodded. Bobby could be manic. I found it best to glide in his slipstream.

"Today we are outlaws, my friend."

I yawned and echoed the word of choice back at him. That was all he wanted after all and I was still surfacing, approaching the median temperament from a way off.

Bobby tugged his sleeve back to reveal elastic bands, crossed and doubled up about his wrist. Holding my eyes - a magician opening the curtain on his big reveal - he slipped the letter opener within, all concealed like.

"We do need summat for you, though," he said, pushing himself up off his haunches and dusting his kecks down.

"I'm alright," I said. "I've got size on my side."

Bobby stopped and looked at me, reappraising. "You have got size. You big lummox. But let's tool you up anyway."

There was a hunk of masonry, probably twice the size of my head, over in the corner which Bobby amused himself with while I pulled on my jeans, lifting, grunting and dropping.

"I'm not carrying a rock," I told him.

"No-one asked you to, did they?"

"I'm just saying is all."

I farted about for what felt like an hour. I knew I was testing Bobby's patience and that gave me a secret thrill. So I brushed my teeth and I rolled up my sleeping bag and shoved it into the back of the fireplace and I had a drink of water and ate three mouthfuls of cold beans I'd left from the night before - Bobby saying, "Cold beans!" in disgust and me answering him with, "What else do outlaws eat?" and I knew I had him there. I asked him if he'd brought me owt and he lobbed me a banana which I ate on the trot because bananas was my favourite.

Wasn't until we were out in the daylight, which was of

that variety – so bright it hurt your eyes, cool enough to raise goosebumps – peculiar to here, that I enquired as to what he had in mind.

"What I have in mind, me old mucker, is to find a mark."

"Amark?" I said, as if Amark was the name of an Indian boy. He got me though.

"Not Amark. You prannock. A – finger space – mark."

We walked on. The factory was at the end of a long street made up of the backs of taller buildings. There were a lot of bins, metal doors, weeds, potholes, graffiti. Nobody came here with any regularity. Bobby often liked to make what he called his coyote calls. But not today. He was intent on something. Being an outlaw gnawing at him. I could tell.

There was a park we liked to hang out in sometimes, a small concrete space at the back of a block of flats. The park had a metal slide, a couple of swings and a long concrete tube that allowed boys to imagine they were marines, scrambling through on knees and urgent elbows, snipers getting in position. I liked to crawl to the middle of the tube and sit with my legs up on the wall opposite me so my feet were higher than my shoulders and close my eyes, something about the coolness of the stone opening me up. I could sit in there for hours. The dark and the cool slowing my brain down to nothing. It was the space that speed came to stop. I thought of it as my brown mood.

A brown mood came on me now, as we walked. Bobby could sense it, I knew, and he left me to it. It was just me getting myself ready for whatever came next.

We walked along a street lined with poplars and Bobby said, "Too many trees."

We walked along a street with houses that had boarded up windows and Bobby said, "Not right."

We walked along a high street mostly made up of charity shops and I could see Bobby mentally checking people off, "No. No. No. No. No. No. No."

I said I was hungry again and Bobby produced a Weight Watchers Brownie Crunch bar he'd stole off of his mum.

"That hardly touched the sides," I said.

Manchester

We walked across the precinct and Bobby said, "Too many cameras."

We took the stairs and loitered upon the upper levels, ducking in and out of the car park and the lifts and TopShop and HMV and McDonalds where I half-inched three chicken nuggets from a lady who was all distracted, cleaning up her baby's milky sick.

"Proper outlaw status now," I said.

Bobby frowned and told me to shut up.

We walked up the long hill into the market and Bobby said, "Still not right."

Bobby spotted his gran, who was a tiny lady with a head no larger than a raisin, so we ducked into Ahmed's and pretended to be actually interested in what clothes girls would wear.

"Yes," Bobby said. "I do believe that neon pink is the next big thing."

I laughed my henchman laugh.

It wasn't until the afternoon that Bobby nudged me in the ribs and said, "Here she comes."

There was a lady about a half a street ahead of us. We were in amongst houses by this point but not family houses, houses carved up into flats with big picture windows and small gardens facing the street. I was sortof lolloping along by this point. My feet were hurting and I felt tired some more. We tailed her for a bit which became a game in itself. She was thrift store chic. Even we knew that. Her coat and her boots and her hat didn't match. From behind she could have been about 70 but when she stopped to cross over and we saw her from the side we thought she was maybe half that.

"We could still have her, though, if she puts up a fight," Bobby whispered.

She didn't walk fast, the lady. She seemed angry at the air. We saw her swatting at the mayflies. We closed the gap. Bobby said, "You grab her. I'll grab her bag. When I say go, we run."

I nodded and licked my lips, which were dry.

"Say it back."

"I grab her. You grab the bag. When you say go, we go."
"Where do we go?"
"We just run until you say."
"Good lad."
"And we stay together."
"That's right. We always stay together."
"Never leave a man behind."
"*Never leave a man behind.*"

We were maybe a car length away when Bobby began with his, "Scuse me, love." We know she heard because she looked over her shoulder at us and we saw her milky blue eyes which were something, I'll tell you. She was ravaged but her eyes were something else. Didn't stop, though. She drew the loop of her bag up over her shoulder and set to a little quicker. Bobby did the bus walk, skipping between steps. "Scuse me, missus. I don't suppose" -

He didn't have to finish. I was sick of all the messing about and just lunged for her. I took her shoulders in my hands and shook her and then I looped my left arm across her chest and held her to me. That was when I noticed the smell of her. Adhesive. *Blue glue*, I thought.

"Hau ab," the lady cursed. Then: "Get. Off. Me."

Bobby stuck his letter opener inches from her face.

"Give us your bag," he said.

"Leck mich," she said and tried to spit at Bobby only the spit didn't travel and ended up decorating my arm.

"You dirty cow," I said, jerking her closer to me. "Ladies don't spit."

Bobby held his letter opener against her neck and threatened to cut her. She went to kick him and missed. Her next move was to try and stamp on my feet. I wasn't having that and so I put my other arm around her waist and lifted her off the ground. The lady's voice rose in pitch and she said what sounded like, "Mist!" That didn't stop me, though. Why would it? I shook her like she was a bottle of pop. While I was doing that I could see Bobby wrestling with the bag saying, "Give it, give it, give it," and the lady clutching on for dear life and making all kind of what sounded like threats in a weird machine gun language I didn't understand.

It took Bobby using the handle of the letter opener against her knuckles to get her to drop it and even then the handbag hit the ground and shit spilled out before Bobby managed to get a good grab and I could drop her like a sack of spuds.

We legged it.

"This had better be worth it," Bobby panted two streets along, his face mottled and red.

"She stank," I said, slowing, the flats of our feet noisy on the pavement.

"Yeah," Bobby gasped. "What was that?"

"She was dirty," I said. "I think we robbed a tramp."

"Her bag is fucking heavy, I'll tell you that."

A car passed and we both had a psychic flash and thought police. It wasn't police, it was a Ford Focus but we had a second wind and ran for another couple of streets until we spied a side road that led to a dog walker's park, a square of greenery surrounded on all sides by common or garden houses. Two ups and two downs. Windows full of shite. No dog walkers about, though. We headed for the sole bit of greenery, a stubby Cedar tree with roots that stuck up out of the ground.

We sat side by side, our backs against the tree. Bobby raised an invisible glass and waited for me to do the same. When I did, we chinked and Bobby said, "To two brave fellows. Outlaws both. Bold and true and loyal to the end."

I grinned, enjoying the fellowship and then Bobby started to root in the bag.

"That explains the heavy," he said placing a large Nescafe jar filled with two pees on the dry earth between us. It said MERCY on the lid, which made us feel bad for a quarter second.

"Do you think it's a church collection thing?" I said.

Bobby mulled and then shrugged.

Next he pulled out a blackened spoon, its head violently twisted to the right.

"Phor. Sniff that," Bobby said passing it to me.

I sniffed and said, "Phor."

"What is that?" Bobby asked as I held it up like a talisman.

"Just burned," I answered him, flicking it into the tall grass. "No use to us."

Bobby took to dropping small items on the ground: a lighter, a transparent bag with a couple of pills in, some receipts, a glove, a ticket stub, a lipstick, some concealer, a ribbon with what looked like flecks of blood on, a library card, a phone bill and an empty paper pharmacy bag that had once contained a prescription for Methadone.

"Is that it?" I asked.

Bobby tipped the bag upside down and a scrunched note fell out.

"Old ladies always do that," I told him.

"Do what?" he said, grunting as he reached for the ball.

"Scrunch up their money at the bottom of their bags."

"Result," he said.

And then there she was, her hand in Bobby's hair, a fistful of what looked like syringes held at his throat.

"You nasty boys," she said, kneeling in the dirt alongside us.

I pushed myself away with my hands and my feet and said, "Sorry lady."

"Never mind your sorry lady," she said in a voice that was at once brittle and determined, her milky eyes ferocious and wide.

"Where is your ridiculous blade?" she whispered in Bobby's ear.

He extended his arm and flapped his sleeve and it dropped on to the ground.

"Throw it a-*vay*," she said.

Bobby gingerly felt for the letter opener and cast it out of the magic circle.

Then she turned her attention to me and I noticed for the first time how terrible her teeth were, yellow and brown and twisted and missing.

"Pick up all of my things please or I will hurt your little

friend in ways that he will not quickly forget."

Bobby grunted and squirmed. The lady moved her hand in such a way that his head tipped further back.

I couldn't take my eyes off the needles at Bobby's throat. There were eight of them presiding over a gentle lattice of scratches.

"Quickly now," she said. "Or my hand will get tired."

I pushed myself up and started to scrabble about, stuffing her treasures, along with small twigs and tufts of grass, back into the bag.

"Little boys," she said. "Silly little boys."

I got everything but the spoon. I didn't like to ask but.

"Bobby. What did we do with the spoon?"

"How the" -

He took an anxious breath. I imagined the needles pressing against his throat a teensy bit harder than they had moments before. The lady was smiling at me like one of the Evil Dead.

"Don't know, mate. Don't know."

I took to kicking at the tall grass, taking a measure of pleasure in the way it snapped off about my feet.

"I don't *haf* all day," she said, jerking Bobby's head back hard, his eyes facing up into the branches of the tree.

"I'm doing my best, lady," I said, her handbag in my hand, bouncing against my leg.

"Do better," Bobby yelled and she laughed, or rather barked. A short sharp exclamation of pleasure.

"Oh dear," she said, gazing lovingly into Bobby's eyes as if he was beloved. "In der not frisst, der teufel fliegen."

"What she says," Bobby called.

I kicked harder at the grass.

"It's not here!"

And then it was, glinting dully amongst the green. I snapped it up, slung it in the bag and then stood, as far from the mad bag lady as I could manage, holding it out to her.

"Bring it," she said.

I looked at Bobby but didn't move.

"Bring it," she said more firmly, "or I will finish your

friend and start on you."

I drew closer and held out the bag to her. She rose to her feet and brought Bobby slowly with her.

"Thank you. We are now going to walk to the street where we will say our goodbyes."

She jerked her chin to suggest I lead the way. I could tell from the thin gasps Bobby was making that the syringes were still at his throat.

"C'mon lady," I said. "You've had your fun."

"I've had my fun?" she said. "You think this is fun?"

"Yes," I answered her, knowing somehow in my blood that she did find it fun.

She chuckled.

"Perhaps you are right at that."

I passed out of the small field, walking along the path that led back to the street as if I was at the head of a funeral cortege, walking with the step/half-step that indicated dignity in some cultures.

I knew she'd freed Bobby when he pinwheeled by me and disappeared off along the street. I didn't follow immediately, turning to her and facing up to her with whatever bravery I could summon.

"You boys," she said, holding her chin up. "You should watch how you play. It's a dangerous world, you know?"

And with that, she turned on her heel and walked away from me, taking what was left of my boyhood with her.

Sarah-Clare Conlon

Sarah-Clare Conlon

Flight Path

I. *Chorlton*
One for Sorrow

No houses in the garden village are completely alike. Number 73 stands on its own at a bend in the road. Number 73 has a woodshed, fully stocked. It has a large garden that stretches towards the river and enough bright light to produce a gleaning amount of vegetables and fruit. It has apple trees and pears and damsons down at the bottom. Raised beds for potatoes and carrots and onions. Number 73 just went on the market. A good price, by all accounts.

After finishing at the school beyond the houses, beside the park, Mrs Benson spent her first couple of weeks digging out the hybrid roses; replacing them with marigolds to fend off slugs and sowing seeds for a self-sufficient future for herself and Mr Benson. Mr Benson had been a bank manager. He liked order and functionality and books that balanced. His wife's plans seemed to fit in nicely.

It was Tuesday when Mrs Benson arrived home with her haul from the fishmongers. As she climbed the steps to the front porch, a magpie flew directly at her, then away.

Mrs Benson lugged her bags through to the kitchen, leant on the sink and looked out at the blossom, but there was no blossom to look at. It had gone. The trees were gone. The apples, the pears, the damsons – there were no longer any near the house, just a huger sky than Mrs Benson had ever known while washing up.

Mr Benson waved over from the woodshed, mouthing "winter".

Mrs Benson nodded slowly and turned the latch on the back door. She walked past the piles of branches and trunks laid neatly on the lawn, sap shining in the blue blue sky of an April noon. She picked up the chainsaw and proceeded towards her husband.

45

II. *Didsbury*
Two For Joy

I would pack a book, whichever I was reading, and sandwiches I had made the night before and laid side by side in a fake Tupperware box which snapped shut on all four sides. I would follow a different route to the weekend, when we went together. Then, we would pass the avenue of poplars where parakeets skittered across the sky, up past the spring where the well was dressed in years gone by but the water still dribbled out. Then, we would come up from down beside the river, up from the old salt road, as I'd heard it called, up the lane that was prone to flooding and so was no longer a right of way to motorised vehicles.

Beyond the heavy steel barrier they shut in times of high rainfall, the trees either side of the track touched branches at the top, no crown shyness, so it felt like a tunnel. Fine when you had a hand to hold, but not with just the magpies for company, so on my own I would take the traffic-noisy option, along the pavement to the ancient village green and the Gates of Hell, where the two inns stood.

"Many entered but were turned aside by temptation, few went on to the church," it was said.

"The road to heaven is paved with good intentions."

The hawthorn alongside the college railings smelt of hymn books.

At weekends, we would stroll in front of the Parsonage and enjoy the corona imperialis lilies and the snake's head fritillaries in the bulb lawn with its signs to not walk. We would kiss beneath the tree with the ball of mistletoe and laugh at our superstitions. I would ask if he'd like to do a circuit in the old vegetable garden and he'd say, no, that's for you, then on Tuesday, I would go there on my own.

It caught the sun, and I would sit and read my book and eat my sandwiches. But first I would go into the Alpine House and sip the air and watch the oversized fish mooching in the small pond with its miniature waterfall. It was cool in there, yet full of scent, the plants just misted; the sedums and the sempervivums. The louvered windows were left slightly ajar, so heat and condensation didn't build up. Not like any glasshouse I had known. Not like the University's Botanical Gardens, hidden in the middle of student land further towards town, nor the secret place at Broomfield Hall, a stone's throw away – not that you would throw stones, of course. But, in any case, hardly any distance as the crow flies.

That day, that Tuesday like any other, I wrote my name and the date in the comments book, as I did every visit, remarking in pencil how well the plants were doing, and remarking to myself that no one had added an entry since my last time here. Not that this would ever surprise me; the greenhouse was only open to the public once a week and I rarely saw anyone other than the gardeners.

I smiled at the volunteer holding aloft a ring of keys as she wandered over to lock up for lunch. I heard the door being pulled to, the bottom dragging on the stone flags, as I went past the dying laburnum hybrid planted by a Frenchman and the camellias shedding their pink tears onto the borders. The giant magnolia tree beckoned me over, and I sat down, bathed in sunlight.

The scraping of rakes and scutching of spades had stopped, almost without me noticing, and I dug into my bag and retrieved my sandwich box. Opening it, I placed it next to me on the bench, under the still shiny plaque remembering someone who had also loved this spot. I wondered about having a bench organised for me on the event of my exit, but there was no space left to squeeze one in, and it didn't seem right somehow to pre-empt your own demise like that.

"Do you get bothered by ghosts much?" I thought I heard a voice say.

A voice says: "Do you get bothered by ghosts much?"

I turn and see a woman with a strange face. Pinched, angular, pale, yet somehow exotic, with wide eyes and heavy lipstick that is bleeding into the fine lines around her mouth. She has alighted on the bench next to me, though I didn't hear her arrive. If I put down my sandwich, I could reach out and touch the blue sleeve of her coat.

"No." I say. "Not that I know of."

"Even here?"

"Why here?" I reply.

"Because there are tales, many, of ghosts. Look across the way there; it wouldn't be too much of a stretch of the imagination."

I look over the bottom lawn, past two sandstone walls and into the churchyard, made sacred to bury plague victims. There are more places to tie up your bike than there are tombstones, but I can make out the family vault of a wealthy cotton man who lived in a now-gone enormous house nearby. The church is the oldest building around, and I look back at the Old Parsonage, which is the second. It has never housed a parson, only the odd visiting curate, and – some locals might have it – a ghost or two.

"The ghosts are just stories," I say to the woman, but when I look back to her, she's gone. A pearly feather lies where she was sitting. I pick it up and put it in my pocket. As I pack my things and stand, I wonder why I didn't notice her leave.

The main house is still open, the little hanging wooden sign tells me as I walk along the path, so I go inside. I catch sight of my reflection in the mirror on the mahogany coatstand inside the front door and adjust my hat – the peacock's eye has gone skew-whiff. I venture up the creaking stairs to the office, announcing my presence with my feet.

"Do you get bothered by ghosts much?" I ask the warden, who looks up from his leather-topped oak desk.

It's a warm place, he tells me.

But the stories, I say.

They're just stories, he answers, and recounts the rational explanations casting doubt over the supernatural: untamed twigs tapping on the roof tiles; mice on twine pulleys making the servants' bells ring in the middle of the night; wind screeching through a broken pane of glass shrill as a tortured woman; the bobby on the beat whispering at the scullery window to get the kitchen maid's attention.

As I leave, I hear a shriek from near the yew tree, then scrabbling in the fallen leaves. I quicken my pace towards the entrance guarded by the calcified spread eagle, but am stopped in my tracks as a jay hops in front of me, cocks its head and stares, before taking flight. An iridescent feather floats down and lands at my feet. It is the same as the one in my pocket. I pick it up and put it with the other, then carry on, back the way I came this morning.

Anthony Trevelyan

Anthony Trevelyan

Repossession

Dolores hears things. It is where she works, he thinks, who she sees. By the prickling glow of the fairy lights she has tied into the frame of her small, stout metal bed she tells him that night some new people came into the bar, a man and two women, and they were very charming and interesting and after a while they began to tell everyone in a friendly way about the secret truth of the city. (At this point he wants to say there is no secret truth of the city – no secret truth of anything – but he only nods and widens his lips.) They said the city is not what it seems, not in its bones, irradiated by history. Far from it. There are groups, they said, cabals, arcane councils that wage unseen and immemorial war upon one another through the streets and buildings and even the people of the polis. A road closure here, a tower-block demolition there: not incidences of everyday urban banality – though of course that's what they're *meant* to look like – but blows, salvos, assaults by one esoteric committee on another in a conflict older than the dinosaur bones of the original encampment.

'Do you think any of it is true?' she asks him, swiftly adding, 'I don't.' But she goes on smiling at him, with steady lambent force, awaiting an answer.

'I think I'd *like* it to be true.' Karl frowns. 'To an extent.'

'Ah yes, but to *which* extent?'

The previous Friday night in a bar two streets away from their building – not the bar where Dolores works – an argument between two men who had never met before culminated in one of the men cutting off the other's hand with a machete. The incident has been much on Karl's mind. Guiltily he is aware that his dread is not what might have happened if these men had met for the first time in the bar where Dolores does work; it is what might have happened if he had himself been present in that bar. He has, after all, stopped by for a drink there on many Friday nights, and his awareness of this fact somehow translates into a sinister tingling that envelopes and horribly isolates his right hand

and wrist. He has no idea which hand it was the victim lost. It may have been his right. But it may as well have been his left.

The city is not what it seems. Well, Karl thinks, he could live with that, if what the city seems now is a severed hand among the glasses on a table in a bar on a Friday night.

★

Where he works is the October Bank, and who he sees is people in critical debt.

The morning's case is in every regard typical. The Mahmoods live in a three-bedroom house in a brackeny cusp of green Didsbury. Amir, forty, a graphic designer, self-employed, prone to wild variation in income, months of drought interrupted by an occasional bonanza, is the husband. Chloe, thirty-eight, a masters student and an entrepreneur, is the wife. Rashi, seventeen, an A Level student, is the son.

'I'm not being funny,' Chloe says when he has been there a little while, 'but I think it's a joke. Honest to God, it's *laughable*.'

It is not a joke. Is it? Eighteen months earlier Chloe opened a bakery on Didsbury High Street. In order to do so, she took out a loan with a bank – not October, not the bank Karl works for. But Amir took out a loan too, and he took it out with October.

Eleven days after its opening, Chloe's bakery closed. Both loans vanished incalculably into the void, the whirlpool of this closure. Though it has nothing to do with him, Karl knows anecdotally that Chloe has not managed to pay off even the first fraction of her debt – has scarcely tendered a goodwill gesture. Amir, by startling contrast, has tried very hard to honour his obligations. But it has not been enough, not nearly enough, and now the bank, incarnated in the person of Karl, is making its house call.

'You have to say these things, of course,' Amir says, the many creases and pleats and folds of a complicated smile distorting his face. It is a face that knows disaster, and sets this distortion against it. 'But there's still time, yes? Just this week I've had commissions coming in left, right and centre. I mean, in reality, we're not going to lose the house, are we?'

Invisibly Karl stiffens. The fearful question. They may say different but they all fear it, all the October agents who work with people in critical debt. Karl knows the case and he knows any hope he offers the Mahmoods will be false. They will lose their house. Nothing, no turn of events, no windfall commission, can prevent that now.

'Don't bother,' Chloe tells her husband. 'What's the use of asking *him*? It's not up to him. He'll say anything. Anything his dark overlords tell him to.'

Rashi, the son, sits in the middle of the couch, between his parents. He has one arm round his father, one round his mother. And for some time after he leaves all Karl can see when he thinks of the Mahmoods is the boy's hands, softly plying his parents' flesh with rhythmic, repeating caresses.

★

'Have you seen my white jeans?' Dolores wants to know.

'Do you have white jeans? Does anyone?'

'Shows what *you* know,' she sighs mysteriously and goes on stalking round the flat, her flat, the flat of which she is at any rate the primary tenant and in which she has lived for five years, into which he moved with her six weeks ago.

It is, in Karl's opinion, rather a decent flat, far preferable to the house share in Ancoats that was, even before he left it, at the point of some radical unravelling. It is slotted into a large grand old building that used to be a department store. Traces of that former life run everywhere through its spaces: the bolted crossbeams, the concrete pillars that transpierce the whole structure like segments of a tremendous skeleton. Dolores has even said, fancifully, at night, before he moved in, she would sometimes intuit 'presences' in the flat, hear snatches of muted conversation, the gossip of counter girls on a break, a boy's name, the story of a bruise, see the bright blur of a figure moving quickly, purposefully across the bedroom, its arms full of something. In a spirit of inquiry he asked her if she was ever frightened by these presences and she said no, it was quite nice, really. Like company.

Half an hour later she reappears looking, he thinks, like a dentist or a mental patient. She is dressed entirely in white – white cardigan, white T-shirt, white jeans, socks, even a pair of white plimsolls so new she must have bought them that evening on her way home from the bar. She crooks her arms and tilts her head, marionette-style, and asks, 'How do I look?'

'Very clean.' It is true. She looks that also.

'Do you think? I think I look like a mad person. Anyway, dress code, so what am I going to do.' And she tells him: she is going to a party with that man and those women who came into the bar last week and started talking about the secret truth of the city. Not, it transpires, a fancy-dress party. 'Everyone just goes dressed like this.'

'Sounds fun.'

'Well, we'll soon see about that.'

Far earlier than he was expecting, not long after midnight, she arrives back at the flat. Still in her white underwear she topples down next to him onto the bed.

'How was it?'

'Silly. Sort of fun, yes, I know, as you said, but totally silly. Insurmountably silly. And I got stuck by this one guy who couldn't stop talking about Andy Burnham.'

'Is he one of these lizard people, too?'

On the pillow she looks at him with silent, mirthful incredulity. As if he had just passed a remark of the most mindless, the most uneducable stupidity.

'Oh,' Dolores says, '*oh*. You wouldn't have liked it at all.'

★

The next time he visits the house is empty. Redundant TV and fibre-optic cables spread over the floorboards in flails. Everything that was going to happen has happened.

Anthony Trevelyan

It is smiling Amir who answers his knock and who courteously leads him from room to room while he makes his inspection (ticks on his clipboard, clicks on his phone). None of the other Mahmoods appears to be at home.

'Where is everyone?' Karl asks, then frowns at himself. It is not in the least his business where the Mahmoods are. It would not usually occur to him to assume it was.

But Amir answers cheerfully: 'Chloe's at the new place, which is actually her dad's. We're going to be staying with Chloe's dad for a while. Could be better, could be worse.' He does not mention the boy, Rashi, however.

As he prepares to leave, Amir's hesitant manner stalls him in the hallway. With a nod that seems largely internal Amir says, 'You shouldn't feel bad. I know you did everything you could for us.'

It is not true. Karl has done nothing for the Mahmoods other than file their paperwork, instalment by missed instalment. He is alarmed, oddly, to discover that Amir has regarded him as some hero agent – fighting the good fight, standing up for the little or common man.

'Everything will get better,' he says uneasily.

'Yes.' Amir reaches towards him with both hands. Before he quite comprehends what has happened Karl has extended a hand in return, his right, and Amir's two hands have closed round it. Tightly. Containingly. 'You're right, of course. All this will pass.'

'A temporary setback.'

'Yes, yes.' Amir's two hands squeeze Karl's. Suddenly and vividly he is confronted by a flashing image of the structure of the bones of his own hand, the ghostly wipe of an X-ray. Then Amir nods again and releases him and Karl's hand is returned to his body, wide and pink and curiously bird-like and somehow negligible. At once he puts the hand in his pocket, as if for safe keeping.

'Take care, Amir. You'll be back on your feet in no time.'

'On my feet or off my rocker. Remember I said we're staying with Chloe's dad!'

Manchester

★

It occurs to him that he cannot remember when he last saw Dolores wearing an item of clothing that was not white. Yes, she wears white when she goes out with these new friends of hers; but at some point it came to pass that she would wear white all the time. He has an idea she wears white during her shifts at the bar. There she is now, on the other side of the couch, ten o'clock on a Saturday morning, reading the paper, wearing white.

'These people you go out with,' he says, abruptly. 'I've just realised I don't know any of their names.'

'Why would you want to know their names?' She chuckles darkly, not looking up from the article she is reading. 'They don't really have names. Or not ones they've told me, anyway. But they have these nicknames. Aliases, if you like. So there's Hobie, and Tula, and Magda…'

'And what sort of group are they?'

'Who says they're a group?'

'Are they not?'

'They're a sort of group. They call themselves – wait for it, you'll love this – they call themselves "The Children of Peterloo". Don't you love it?'

'I do.' Aliases. The city is not what it seems. The Children of Peterloo. 'In fact, I love it so much I think it's high time I met these friends of yours.'

'What?' Now she does look at him. 'You want to come out with us?'

For an instant he does consider it. But no: the thought is too terrible. 'Or I could stay in with you. With them. Do you think you could persuade them to come round?'

'Here?'

'Why not here?'

She stares at him. It is, as ever with Dolores, a stare that has a great deal going on in it – wheel turns, pendulum swings. At last, slowly, she lifts her shoulders and narrows her eyes and wrinkles her nose. 'You'd have to wear white.'

'I think I could manage that.'

Anthony Trevelyan

★

It is Friday night and he is walking back from a bar – not the one where Dolores works – to the flat, coursing along through the noise and mass and sense of rupture that is Thomas Street on a Friday night. He is not drunk, not very drunk, and he steps fairly nimbly round the various staggered friezes of human concourse he encounters in his path.

Up ahead he glimpses a familiar face, and he is already breaking into a smile, getting ready to hail a pal or a colleague, when he realises the face is familiar because it is the face of Rashi Mahmood.

The boy is standing in the road, without friends, it appears, a bulky rucksack tightly strapped to his back. And this, it appears, is how he is afraid, this freezing light moving over his guts, this is how mortal fear presents itself, because Rashi has seen him too and he is fifteen or even twenty paces ahead and even if Karl immediately starts to run the young man still has all the time he could need to shrug the rucksack from his shoulder and take from it whatever he has stowed inside it – a knife, a machete, anything.

Karl does not start to run. He tells himself that Rashi will look away, that if he looks away the young man will look away. He looks away. But even now that he is no longer looking he knows Rashi has not looked away.

He will shout – Rashi will shout at him. *You. You reckon you some big man? You ain't no big man. You ain't nothing.* But Rashi does not shout at him.

Karl looks again and now he sees Rashi, looking straight at him, crossing to intercept him. Ducking his head but not taking his eyes off the teenager, Karl veers hurriedly to the right. But Rashi veers too, and raises his arms at his sides, as if making ready to tackle him.

Karl stops walking. Rashi stops also, directly in front of him. All about them Thomas Street churns in its parallelograms. With a spring Rashi dives at him. Distractedly now Karl raises his arms too but the boy catches him easily by both wrists.

He can see nothing but Rashi Mahmood's face and its weird expression (intense, but bereft of the usual markers of violence). Rashi's eyes scan his face continually, as if examining it for signs of disease or distress.

'It's not you,' Rashi says. His voice is full of breath. 'Don't let them tell you it's you.'

'What?' Karl thinks he says. It is not certain he says anything.

'Whatever they make you do. You don't become it. You don't have to become it.'

The boy blinks and leans forward and lightly kisses him on the forehead and then the pincer-grips suspending Karl's wrists snap loose and the next thing he sees is Rashi's back as he walks away, Rashi's back and his rucksack full of textbooks and all the notepads and pencils of a student so outlandishly diligent he has spent his Friday night in the library.

★

'How do I look?' Karl asks.

He crosses back from the bedroom into the sitting room of the flat wearing fluffy white slippers, billowing white pyjama bottoms and a deeply V-necked white T-shirt that has gained a bluish tinge in the wash, like a shadow that cannot detach from it.

But Dolores is nervous, and hardly glances at him. 'Weird,' she says flatly.

He decides not to press it. And then The Children of Peterloo arrive.

Hobie is a slight, silver-haired man of about Karl's father's age. He shakes hands with Karl, then with Dolores, then with the other two women, then finally with himself, and laughs theatrically, showing dark metal in his back-teeth.

Tula is perhaps a little younger (about Karl's mother's age). She has an intent frivolous gaze and wears her hair long and straight and tends somewhat vainly to flip it about, to show off its zigzags of glamorous grey.

The last of the three, Magda, is much younger (Dolores' age? Younger?). She has no hair to speak of and her face seems all lugubrious and lidded eye. The sort of person to whom the word 'owlish' should attach, though for some reason, he cannot quite tell why, it does not.

'Well,' Karl says when the three guests have settled into their directed places on the couch and he, under Dolores' scattered direction, has brought each of them a tumbler of water, 'it's nice of you to come.'

'It was nice of you to invite us,' Tula says, with mocking blandness.

'Wonderful to make your acquaintance, Karl, *Karl*.' Hobie seems to roll his name round his mouth. 'Dolores has told us so much about you.'

'Has she?' Karl has absolutely no notion what Dolores, or anyone, might have to say about him.

'Certainly she has. About your interest in us. In our ideas, our preoccupations.'

'Well,' Karl says again. 'They do sound interesting.'

'It is no small thing to confront the truth. I've always said that. Not that it agrees with everyone. Plenty of folk are much better off not coming within a hundred miles of anything true. That's the trouble with it, the truth. It's dangerous. Explosive, even.'

'Yes,' Karl says. 'I suppose I can see that.'

'Can you, though?' There is nothing sharp in Hobie's voice or manner, yet Karl feels a great magnitude of attention somewhere seizing on him. 'Are you sure you want to know about them? I trust you know who I mean when I say *them*?'

'The lizard people,' Karl says for some reason.

Tula laughs with sour uncontrollability. But Hobie only continues mildly to smile at him.

'That's right, Karl, *Karl*. The lizard people.'

'And that's what you have in common, is it?' Karl steers his glass through a loop that includes the three of them. 'Knowledge of these groups?'

'You might say that,' Hobie allows. 'Knowledge. Yes, that might be it.'

'And we're all dead,' Magda says. 'There's that as well.'

Gradually Hobie begins to laugh, then Tula begins to laugh, then all three of them are laughing, and yes, it is what it appears to be, a young woman's awkward joke.

'Yes,' Hobie says. 'There's that as well.'

They have barely left when Dolores comes at him with her eyes wide and both hands over her mouth. He worries that something is seriously wrong until she releases a sort of hot shout through her fingers and says with sudden squawking recklessness, 'Oh my God they're *mad*, aren't they? Obviously, I always knew they were mad, but it was only just now I realised *how* mad. They're *crackers*.'

'Maybe,' Karl says.

'All that stuff. "We do not as we wish, but as we are wished". "Your mind is not your mind, but their tool. Your body is not your body, but their weapon". Christ, it's like waking up after a bender or something. How did I not *realise*?'

'I don't know. I think we left the door open.'

'Did we?'

He goes to the door, stands frowning at it. Then he steps outside and they are there in the gloom of the hallway, three white ghosts patiently waiting at the top of the stairs. Hobie, smiling, raises a hand to him. Tula flips her hair. Magda only looks at him – looks and looks. Strange, Karl thinks. The three of them. What they seem and not what they seem at all. After another moment he closes the door quietly behind him and crosses the hallway to where they are standing and one after the other they start to make their way down the steep stairs.

Bryony Bates

Coleoptera

The first pollinators were beetles, before bees and wasps,
crawling between flowers…
Two-hundred-and-seventy or three-hundred-and-eighty
million years ago, crawling, older than flowers
They are found in almost every habitat except the sea and
the Polar Regions.
"I see very few these days"
New species are discovered frequently
"The beetles are disappearing."

Appear: "to come forth, be visible; submit, obey,"

"The beetles are disappearing here in Australia. I see very few
these days, compared to the huge numbers from my youth.
from suffixed form of PIE root ★yeu- "vital force;
In Middle English, the -g- became a yogh,
which then disappeared.
Who keeps a dead tree?

★sek-
meaning "to cut." secare "to cut,"
seko, sešti "to cut,"
sech' "to cut;"
doescim "I cut."
★sken- "to peel off, flay"
extended form of ★sek- "to cut."
Sclerotin is formed by cross-linking members of particular
protein molecules,
a biochemical process called sclerotization
sclerosis (n.)
"a hardness, hard tumor," from Greek sklerosis "hardening"
"morbid hardening of the tissues"
Technically, this amounts to a form of tanning

Manchester

All the carnall beauty of my wife, Is but skin-deep.
from carnis "of the flesh," derived from caro "flesh, meat,"
"flesh,"
from PIE root *sker- (1) "to cut."
Or "natural, of the same blood,"
And then I was a thing: a body.
Ah but some natural notes about her body
asking for more skin, more sex.
I might call him
A thing divine, for nothing natural
I ever saw so noble.
Which is the natural man, and which the spirit?
Is a joke the same as a lie?

Summers always had many beetles flying against the windows at night,
but now I never see any. What have we done
to all the Earth's creatures.

Scrape (scraping a living): scrape (v.)
probably from Old Norse skrapa "to scrape,
erase," "scrape out, scrape off, shave; abolish, remove,"
"to scrape, scratch, gnaw"). Of magnetic tape
forms all or part of razor, rat
Of these there are the following kinds:
a black rat and a grey rat, a py-rat and a cu-rat
To cure and conjure – curious
See what happens when you tickle a rat
Here's the sound it makes when you tickle its back
They can ruin your food, destroy things in your home
and start electrical fires.
Rats and their fleas can carry disease.
Can you kill them with baking soda?
Where Do Rats Live Outside?
Under wood piles or lumber
Under bushes and vines
In grasses that are not trimmed or cut back
Under rocks in the garden

In holes under buildings
In cars, appliances, furniture
In and around trash that's been left on the ground
Do Not Give Food And Shelter
To These Most Unwanted Guests!
Consuming the plaster of Paris will kill them when it combines with fluids and hardens in their
gastrointestinal tracts.
Rats!

"So the difference between a joke and a lie is that one flouts Gricean maxims and one violates them. Even if someone doesn't get the joke, or doesn't notice the joke, the question isn't whether they did get it but whether they were expected to.
Try to make your contribution one that is true.
"The listener onscreen is not expected to get the joke but we as members of the audience are.
Make your contribution as informative as is required
Which could also be true in real world conversation."
Be relevant.
"Maybe they just *don't* lie because they've been told that they can't"
Avoid obscurity of expression/Avoid ambiguity/Be brief
I think that's how it works, but I'm not a linguist."

Be orderly.
I think that's how it works.

The rat is normal taking a shower,
he is not running around desperately.
Do I bother you every time you eat rat's meat or dog's meat at some restaurant?

"The dogs were just so sweet.…They just want a connection. They just want some attention,"

Entomophagy is the name for eating insects

Manchester

Most insects are 100% edible,
compared with about 40% of a cow
Many insects are high in calcium, zinc, iron and protein
Beetles make up 40% of all recorded edible insect species

I see nothing intrinsically 'bad' about eating dog.
I see everything bad about
'double standards'//vegans who ignore the SUFFOCATION
of insects and the MUTILATION
of small scurrying animals in the PROCESS
of agricultural production. As we MUST eat foodstuffs that
are alive (like plants)
or formerly alive (like animals) we have little choice.
What choice we do have should be put into caring in advance for what we eat.

Puppies are squeezed into excruciatingly cramped metal cages. They are left alone for most of their lives, yelping for help that never comes #mood.

Excessive Attention Seeking and Drama Addiction – Psychology Today

cynic (n.)
literally "dog-like,"

Valerie O'Riordan

Valerie O'Riordan

Nate

'Get a bloody wriggle on, Nate!' The foreman was shouting at me. 'New bloke's got the march on yeh already, don't he?'

I put my phone away—silent, not off; Imran might still call—and headed across the site.

This week's job was to rip down a year's worth of fly-posted ads before repainting the render on the Bet Or Debt gable wall while Milo and his regulars rewired the inside. The new bloke, hefty-looking on the spindly ladder, was halfway up already and clawing at a poster.

I heaved my way skywards to get a better look. Mid-forties, I reckoned. Thick-legged. Sturdy. Curling hair, longish over the ears and a nice clean neck. He turned. I flinched, tensed for the usual—*piss off, yeh bender*—but all he said was, 'Y'all right, bud?'

I wondered if—

'Here,' he said, 'see this?' He nodded at the poster. A leftover from last year's Council elections: *Sharon Kelly! Vote #1 for Cleaverton North!* He tapped her weather-beaten paper face. 'My missus, innit?'

'Oh,' I said. Disappointed, like. Then, because he was watching me, 'I mean, w-wow. P-politician, is she?'

'Nah.' He thumped her chin. 'Came in last, din't she?'

'I'm s-sorry,' I said, and he said, 'Oh, mate. No need. Those days are long gone.' And he spat off the ladder. Nearly hit the gaffer.

I laughed.

'Here, but,' he said. 'Watch this.' He stamped up a couple of rungs until he was level with her eyeballs. Then he leaned out and clawed at the massive papery helix of her ear: the rip jagged out, as far as the tufty sprig of hair that spiked from her crown. Her face split open, one eye slit in half, the lips flapping. 'Eh? Better?'

'N-nice,' I said.

He grinned and I grinned back.

The gaffer yelled up at us to crack the fuck on.

The new bloke kept pulling. An ad for mincemeat

appeared from beneath the campaign poster: raw coils of meat nestling under his ex-missus's cheekbone like a nest of maggots. He tugged harder. He was out of breath. The exhaust pipes from the traffic below whipped up dirty great gusts of smoke that reeled about him like baby twisters, tearing at his shirttails, uncovering his skin, pink like new plaster.

'L-lovely,' I said.

★

Lunchtime. The pub. The Glory Hole. My local, though I didn't often visit: the Big Liz in Withington was more my scene, but I'd started feeling podgy and ignored in there, and besides, Imran didn't much like it. Mostly I drank at home.

'Tall and short,' said the new bloke. Conn Kelly. He'd got us each a pint of stout and a shot of whiskey. The rest of the crew was out in the smoking lounge. The gaffer, Milo, was at the bar, hassling the girl at the taps. Conn sat down beside me. He said, 'I'll tell you what, though, Nate. It's Nate, in't it?'

I nodded.

'Well. Nate. If Shaz walked in now—like right now? I'd batter her. I fucking would.'

Nod, nod, nod. He'd been on about this all morning. Shaz this, Shaz that. He fucking hated her. He fucking loved her. If he saw her now, he'd fuck her up. If he saw her now, he'd fucking cry. If I saw her now, I thought, *I'd* fucking cry. I took a long drink and stared into the glass.

'Aw, Jesus,' he said. 'You think I'm some sort of vigilante nutjob.'

'N-no,' I said, 'n-not at—'

'Because I'm not, like. I'm a decent skin, Nate. It's messed with my head, is all. I'm just, like—,' and he made a fist, knocked it against his forehead.

'N-no,' I said, 'don't!' I didn't dare to pat him on the arm. But still. I said, 'Yeh'll m-meet somebody else.'

He downed his shot. 'You think?'

'Yeah,' I said. 'Why not, like? L-look at yeh.'

Valerie O'Riordan

A pause. I was flushing. Shit, I thought. Shit shit shit.
Then he laughed. 'Jesus. A right charmer, mate, in't you?'
I smiled at the sticky tabletop.
Then Milo appeared: 'All right, poofters?' he went, and I stopped smiling.
'Go and shite,' said Conn.
'Ah, get a life,' said Milo, 'he's not bothered—are yeh, Nate? Shove up, yeah?' And he sat in between us, spread his legs, slapped me on the shoulder. 'Nobody drinking that?' He picked up my shot and sank it. Then he started up about Everton's chances in the League; Conn said something about City v Arsenal this weekend, and I excused myself—I went and sat in the toilet until it was time to get back to work.

★

Home. Later. The computer firing up, lasagna in the oven. Me in my socks. Gin in a can. A heartbeat bass-line beating down through the ceiling—my upstairs neighbour was the Sunday D.J. at the Big Liz. D.J. RoadKill. I cracked open the can, dialed Imran's mobile. No answer. And again: ditto. I got up, fetched my lasagna. Lukewarm. The cheese crusting up. Ate half of it standing at the worktop, sat back down. Second can. Imran: no reply.

I got up again, walked around. The flat was small—the front half of the first floor of an Edwardian semi overlooking the old Cleaverton bowling green. An okay pick-up zone at dusk if you're stuck. I wasn't stuck. I got a new SIM card out of my wallet. Switched it for the old one. Dialled again. *Zero-seven-nine-one—*

This time he'd get *caller unknown*, not *Nathan Carson*. He'd pick up now. He'd done it before.

But still: three rings. Then four. Five, and I started to worry: what if he'd changed his number? Or what if he was ill—what if he was in hospital? What if he'd been jumped? I put a hand to my nose—the crooked ridge where Jack the Roof had smacked me sideways with a wrench after last year's Christmas do—and felt woozy. *Imran*—

But then he answered: 'S'up?'

And of course I couldn't speak. His voice: I was breathing too hard. My guts went numb. I sat down on the floor. I hung up.

Fuck, I thought, fuck fuck fuck.

Stood up. Sat down. Stood up again—the kitchen. The basin. I retched. The taste of the lasagna. My hands weren't steady. Sat back down—loaded his Facebook page. Stared at the profile picture. Thought, Nate, come on. Come on. Jesus Christ. Talk to him.

I dialed again.

'Terry, mate? That you?' He sounded distracted—I pictured him in his underpants, his students' work spread out over the kitchen table. His own can of gin. 'You're late, bro.'

'Imran,' I said, 'it's m-me. It's Nate. P-please don't—'

He hung up. Not a word—just *click*.

I dialed again. Pick up—hang up. And again. And again, oh God.

The fifth time he said, 'Nate, man, we're not doing this. I've told you.'

'J-just listen—'

'It's harassment, isn't it? Every morning, every night—my family live here, man!'

'Okay,' I said, 'so wh-when—'

Click.

I stared at the phone. Then dialed again. But this time it didn't even ring: the screen said *call failed*. I knew that one. He'd blocked me. Again. Another card, wasted—I slid it out of the phone, stamped on it. Put the other one back in. Finished my can. Sat about a while. Stared at nothing. Barely cried. Finally called St. Jude's: the night matron answered.

'Mrs. Fitz,' I said, 'it's N-Nate Carson here. Just c-confirming Saturday?'

Saturday was Pa's birthday. Seventy-eight years old. I hadn't seen him in near on eighteen months. He had the nurses screen his calls. I kept turning up anyway.

'Nate,' said Mrs. Fitz, 'of course, love. But you know he

might not—'

'Yeah,' I said. 'It's okay.'

'Well,' she said, 'okey-dokey!'

I hung up. Walked the length of the room a couple of times. Then put on my coat on and went out. Downstairs. Crossed the road. Stood at the edge of the green, back to the road.

★

Next day. Work. Conn wasn't in—Milo had sent him to the builders' merchant for pipes and sockets. So I was up the ladder alone to finish the stripping.

Milo yelled: 'Mind yeh don't fall, old man—yer boyfriend ain't here to catch yeh today!'

'F-fuck off,' I said, but he'd already walked away.

Up the ladder. Rip, rip, rip. I started at the top and worked down. Tiny ribbons of Conn's ex-wife still clung to the bricks—fillets of skin, the prong of an elbow. I thought about Imran. He wasn't saying harassment when he'd taken his pants off. What had Conn said? A charmer. I was a charmer.

'That's f-fucking right,' I said, scraping at the tatters of the woman's mouth.

Four o'clock. Milo called time. The rest were off to the Hole. I said I had to get my old man a present and I legged it for the bus to town. The 264 to Piccadilly and the tram to Rochdale. A twenty-minute walk. 1073 Belgrave—as per his driving license. 971. 973. Halfway between the mosque and the Aldi. I chewed Hubba Bubba. There. A fuchsia tree. Net curtains. I rang the doorbell. Nothing.

He'd be back from work by now. He taught I.T. in a local high school. He'd told me about the boys and the knackered equipment and the head teacher's breakdown. It was a ten-minute walk away.

I rang the doorbell.

Nothing.

Nothing.

Manchester

No: footsteps.

I stuck my hands in my pocket. Nonchalant. Coughed. Inhaled.

The door opened—

—on a kid. The brother. Abdul? Abdullah? Fuck. There was a sister and two brothers—the kid and a stepbrother, a cabbie in his twenties. Imran was twenty-nine. No—thirty. He'd be thirty now. Thirty since last month—I should have brought a card. Stupid. Stupid. I'd got his sock, though— he'd lost it under my sofa. I had it in my inside pocket. I gave it a quick rub.

'All right, s-son,' I said, 'I'm here for Imran.'

He put his hands on his hips. He was like ten years old. 'Hey,' he said, 'you're that mental—'

'Abdul! TV room, now!' A woman came out. The sister. She pushed the lad deeper into the house, then jabbed a finger at me. 'Hello? Crazy boy? How many times am I standing here?'

'Is he in?' I said.

She jabbed again. 'He ain't into this, old man. He don't like you.'

'That's n-not true! Imran!' I shouted into the house. 'Imran, I'm here!'

The sister turned and shouted too: 'Bro!'

Well, okay: I smoothed down my jacket.

'All right, son?' A man. A different man—not Imran. A larger bloke. Broader face, pin-stripe jacket, a Man City shirt. 'All right?' he repeated, and he hit me in the jaw.

I fell over. Howled. The pain—Jesus.

'I'll s-sue you,' I said—a garble of wet noise. 'Th-that's assault—th-that's—'

Slam went the door.

★

Milo stared at me. 'What happened you?'

'Root c-canal,' I said.

I'd lost a tooth—a pointy one. I'd drooled blood all night.

My face was swollen up like a rotten plum but I felt okay. I'd downed two of Ma's old Diazepams before leaving the flat. I floated towards the ladder.

'Whoa! Yer not goin' up there like that,' he said, blocking my way. 'I'm not insured for this shit. Oy, Kelly!' He waved Conn over. 'Call this cunt a taxi, yeah?'

Conn stared. 'Jesus Christ, mate, you all right?'

I gave him a salute. 'Aye-aye, captain!' Wobbled. Laughed.

He grabbed my arm. 'Jesus, Milo—he can't manage a taxi! I'm bringing him home.'

'Oh, brilliant! St. John's fucking Ambulance, are we now?' Milo threw up his arms. 'Suit yerselves—yeh know where I am if yer lookin' for actual work.'

'*You're* the cunt,' said Conn, but he was too late: Milo was gone. He steered me across the road. A dirty little Mazda hatchback. Leopard-skin upholstery. McDonald's boxes on the floor. Nuggets. I loved nuggets—I beamed at him.

'Right!' he said. 'Address. Nate? Nate, come on—where do you fucking live, man?'

He dug in my pocket for my wallet. Then whoosh—a woozy turn through the streets—we were home and he was hauling me back out onto the pavement. Up the weedy little graveled path. Keys out, up the stairs, coats off. I fell onto the couch. Smiled at his shadow on the ceiling.

'Mi casa su casa,' I said.

He was looking around. The dishes. The dust clusters. The DVD boxes with the explicit stickers. The saucepan beside the coffee table—last night's piss-pot. He drew back and I laughed. He went into the kitchen. The cupboard doors opened and shut. He came back with an old half-eaten M&S pasta-bake.

'Look,' he said, 'have you somebody I should be calling? Like, family, or—?'

'S'all right,' I said. 'I'm f-fine, in't I?' I yawned and winced. My jaw hurt. The Diazepam packet was over by the TV. I tried to reach it. Toppled off the couch.

'Oh, Christ,' said Conn. He helped me back up. Settled me—cushions, the duvet—and took the pills away. Took them out into the hall. I yawned again. Heard him out there on the phone—*the fuck do you want me to do? He's off his head, I can't just—*

★

I don't know. Later.

'Nate? Nate, come on!' He was trying to sit me up.

I'd spewed in my sleep. Conn was fussing at the couch cushions with a wad of toilet paper. His fingernails were caked with sick. A mess of it on the carpet. There was a stain there already, Ma's red wine, which I'd left. I wiped my mouth on my sleeve.

'I went to the Tesco,' he said. 'Got you some bits.'

Mushroom soup. Bread rolls. A packet of Ginger Nuts, some lemonade, a huge packet of twirly pasta. It was bow pasta I liked. Still though.

'L-lovely,' I said.

He put the biscuits on the mantel. Picked up the photo of Ma and Pa and Joel: 'This the family? They not around?'

'My b-brother's in Tokyo. M-mad place,' I said.

'Oh yeah? You been to Japan?'

'N-naw. P-Pa went. He's in a h-home now,' I added, but he weren't listening—he'd picked up Ma's old carriage clock.

D-don't!' I went, but the other photo fell down anyway. It was Imran asleep. I'd done a printout from my phone at the machine in the library.

'Who's this?'

'N-nobody.'

'Don't look like nobody.' Conn was grinning. 'Looks well fit, he does.'

'It's j-just—'

'Like the younger fellas, do yeh? Eh, Nate, you're a well dark horse.'

'It's c-complicated,' I said, 'all right?' I touched my face where the swelling was worst.

'You what?' He looked again at the picture. The grin was gone. 'It weren't him who done that? Your bloke?'

'W-well—'

'Fuck's sake, Nate! Shit like that—did you call it in?'

'N-naw,' I said. 'It d-don't matter.'

'Like fuck it don't matter!' His face was red. 'Complicated— I'll complicate him, the prick.'

I flushed again. 'C-Conn. Please.' I touched his elbow. 'It's all right.'

'Like fuck it is.' He looked around. 'I need a bloody drink.'

'S-sit down,' I said.

I poured whiskey and lemonade into Ma's picnic beakers. More whiskey than lemonade. He drank his fast and held out for another. Wiping his lips on my tea-towel. I sat down beside him and switched on the TV. The News, though—I hated the News. I went to turn over, but he said, 'No, no, leave it. Please.' He'd put his hand on my arm. The weight of it. The warmth. I stayed still. Barely breathed. The TV went—

—arrests during today's ongoing demonstration highlighting the plight of rough sleepers in—

'There,' he said, 'look. Fuck.'

The Newswoman in her suit loitering beside a patchy old tent. Talking to a tramp in a, what was it—Ma used to have one—a cagoule.

'She's had her hair chopped,' said Conn.

'You what?' I said, but then the TV explained:

—campaigner Sharon Kelly at the scene. Ms. Kelly, what use do you think—

The ex. Well, she looked a state. She looked about as fed up as I felt, with Conn stuck to the screen: he'd shifted forwards on the seat so his hand was off my arm. I got up to pour him another drink and he swallowed it without comment. And another.

Finally, the Weather. Conn stood up, stretched—no, I thought, shit, don't go don't go don't go—and sat back down. He sighed. Yawned. 'Maybe you've the right idea, Nate. Fuck the girls. Keep it simple.'

'It's n-not—,' I began, but he wasn't done: 'Fuck her, anyway,' he said. 'Oh, shit.' He was swaying. Red and now

Manchester

crying.

Right, I thought. Okay. I got up. I went and pulled the duvet off the bed in the other room and brought it in and laid it over him. He curled down obediently and pulled the cover up over his shoulders. Soon enough he was snoring. Easy as, I thought, and I sat on the arm of the couch and—*go on*—patted his shoulder. Nice. I felt pretty good. And then my phone rang. Fuck's sake. I looked at Conn: he'd not stirred. Then I saw the screen:

Imran Hussan.

I didn't answer. I nearly did but then I didn't and then I switched it off—not on standby, either, but proper off. And put it up on the high shelf. I went back to the arm of the couch. Imran, I thought. Imran Imran Imran. But I left the phone where it was.

★

Two a.m.: in bed, couldn't sleep. My gums hurt, my cheeks hurt. Ma's stash was down to a useless baggie of paracetamol. I got up again and went back to the lounge. I didn't know where Conn had put the Diazepam. His coat was on the floor. I checked the pockets: a pencil, his car-keys. No pills. I looked at him—should I try his trouser pockets? Probably not. He'd kicked the duvet halfway off. I watched his chest rise—fall. I touched it. Holding my breath. He didn't stir. I put my hand under the duvet. On his left thigh.

'Well,' I said. 'Conn. H-hello.'

Fuck the Diazepam. Back to the bedroom. I got the laptop from under the bed and opened the browser. New tab. Facebook. CONN KELLY. *Click. Click.* There he was. Smiling. Straddling a paint roller. I looked over through the doorway—his hand dangling like he was reaching out. Fuck Imran. Back to the computer. *Request friend.* And: *Click. Save photo as.*

★

Saturday morning. He was up. Filling the kettle in his t-shirt and boxers. He showed me his phone: he'd texted Milo—*any work?*—and Milo had texted back: *piss off!!*

Conn said, 'Screw him, anyway. I could do with a break. My head's a wreck.'

He poured me a bowl of Shredded Wheat. I watched. Here he was, still. Boiling the kettle in his—

The doorbell rang.

Conn looked at me.

'P-postman,' I said.

'I'll get it,' he said. 'You look rough as fuck—no offence.' He went out into the hall and I got down the tea bags. The buzzer clicked. Half a minute later: the knock on the inner door. Conn undoing the chain, saying, 'All right, bud, just a sec.'

Then: 'Uh—is Nathan in?'

I dropped the tea bags.

Conn went, 'You're that bloke he told me about. Aren't you? Bud, you've got some fucking nerve.'

I got to the hall. Breathless already.

'Nathan!' Imran looked confused. 'Who's this geezer?'

I hadn't time to squish myself in between them before Conn went, 'Your worst fucking nightmare, mate,' and belted Imran across the face. There was a grunt and a splodgy little *thwack*. Imran shrieked—a high, pained, *Ngggg!*—and fell back against the wall, hands to his nose.

'Oh, G-God!' I shoved past Conn. 'Imran! S-say something!'

'F-fuck off!' he gurgled, and twisted away.

'Hey!' Conn pulled my arm. 'What are you doing?'

'Seeing if he's okay! His f-face—'

'His face? What about your bloody face?'

'I t-told you it's complicated!'

'Complicated! If *my* bloke slapped me around—'

'Oy!' Imran. 'I'm not his bloke.' He was nasal. Wet-mouthed. He hawked a blob of frothy blood onto the floor. 'And I never—'

'Sh-shut up!' That was me. 'S-stop it!'

'Hold up a sec.' Conn let go of my arm. 'What's going

on here?'

'Nothing's going on!' Imran again. 'Only came all the way over here, didn't I, to see if he was all right. Because I'm a fucking numpty, ain't I?'

Conn looked at me.

I tried to laugh, but it came out a rattled snort. 'Look,' I said, 'just c-come here a minute.' And I beckoned him back into the front room.

He frowned, hesitated, but came with.

'Listen,' he said, 'I have no idea what kind of stupid games yous two are playing, but—'

'W-wait,' I said, and I put my hand on the back of his neck and kissed him.

'Fuck's sake!' He shoved me off. 'What was that for? What's wrong with you?'

'N-nothing!' I tried grabbing his hand, but he snatched it away; he rubbed his mouth, repeating, 'Fuck's *sake*.'

'Wh-what?' I said.

He ignored me. Turned away, paced up and down the room a minute, then came back. 'Nate,' he went, 'that poor fucker out there needs a doctor.'

'S-sit down,' I said. 'I'll m-make that tea.'

'Tea,' he repeated. 'Jesus Christ.' He went back out. Didn't look at me, banged the door shut after himself.

I could hear the two of them talking in the hall. Muttering. Imran and Conn. And me on my own. No tea. No Diazepam. I lay down on the carpet. Shut my eyes. They were whispering out there. Laughing. There wasn't anything at all wrong with me.

'Nate!' Conn. Loud. I sat up. 'Get up, Nate, I said—we're off!'

★

Back in the little grey Mazda. The smell of nuggets, the animal-print upholstery. This time I got to sit up beside Conn in the passenger seat and watch him twiddle with his Satnav while Imran, in the back, pinched his swollen nose and picked at the little red globules of blood that were hardening like burst snot bubbles on his upper lip. Imran and Conn—Conn and Imran. And me. I was grinning.

Conn barked, 'Seatbelts!'

And off we went, down the A6, happy families driving. It was nice out, too—we could be off to the beach. I put the radio on:

—closures due to continuing protests. We spoke to—

Conn flicked it off. He shouted over his shoulder: 'You okay back there, bud?'

A groan. 'Oh, yeah, top dollar, bro.'

Conn said, 'What a fucking morning.'

'Hey,' I said, sitting forward, 'maybe later we could go to—,' and then I stopped: Conn had swung left after a sign for the Royal Infirmary, and we'd shot past the Job Centre and the massive Lidl. 'Oh, shit,' I went, and I grabbed for the wheel; Conn slapped me away, going, 'Jesus fucking Christ, Nate!'

'N-no,' I said, 'you don't g-get it—you have to s-stop!' The car's clock was blinking 11:15. It was Saturday—I'd forgotten. And now I was late, and we'd overshot the turn-off. 'C-Conn, stop!'

'What? No!'

'But my P-Pa—St. J-Jude's!'

'Eh?' said Conn. He glanced at Imran in the mirror.

I twisted around too. 'It's his b-birthday, I have to vi-vi-vi—'

Conn interrupted: 'Nah, nah, nah—look at the state of him back there! This is your mess, man, you're not ducking it.'

'Imran,' I went, 'p-please!'

Imran had his eyes closed. He flapped his hand towards me without opening them. 'Let him the fuck out, man. I don't care.'

I turned back: 'C-Conn!'

A growling sigh from Conn—'un-fucking-believable!'—and then he slapped the indicator knob: *tick-tick-tick* and we swung in a U-turn. A Transit van rounding the next bend braked hard and blasted its horn, but we were already pulling into the cul-de-sac, in to the curb. I'd unbuckled before he stopped.

Conn double-parked. Sat back. Looked at me. Eventually: 'Well?'

'W-well, what?' I said. 'Aren't you c-coming?'

Silence.

Then Imran went, 'Nate. Go on. Get out, man. Go.'

'Okay! Okay.' I looked at them. Imran and Conn. Conn and Imran. 'If you c-came in, though—'

Conn thumped the steering column. 'Nate! Get out of the pissing car already!'

'All right!'

More silence.

'Nate,' went Imran.

'I said all right!' I got out. Shut the door. Crossed the little carpark slowly.

Inside, Mrs Fitz was on the desk. Beyond her—through a locked door—was the Day Room. Old ladies. Old men. Weekend reunions. Kids and grandkids. The tables thick with fliers: prostate checks, hemorrhoid creams. *Have You Written Your Will?*

Mrs. Fitz looked up. 'Nathan, love! Here you are.'

Outside, the Mazda was revving. Belching smoggy puffs. Conn's door opened. Come on, I thought, come on come on *come on*—

She came around to stand beside me. 'I'll swipe you through, pet, shall I?'

He threw a fag butt out onto the tarmac and slammed the door again.

She was patting my shoulder. 'Our Mr. C. was very chipper at breakfast, you know. I think maybe today's your day, pet. Eh?'

The car began to move. It drove away—out of sight down the main road. The empty road. Pigeon shit. A siren whining. Distant traffic and crows and a child somewhere bellowing, 'No! No! *No!*'

'Oh, yeah,' I said. 'D-definitely.'

Thom Cuell

Thom Cuell

Epilogue

I'm sitting in The Salisbury, an old-fashioned rock pub just off Oxford Road. Engles wrote about this place in *The Condition of the Working Class in England*, explaining that the weird angle of Oxford Road train station to the rest of the city was designed to hide the city's slum dwellings, of which this pub is one of the last remaining examples, from the businessmen journeying in from Whalley Range or Chorlton. These small literary echoes resonate around Manchester, a small imaginative map that lies over the territory of Manchester. We've already seen the ghosts of Pinter and Orton, Turing and De Quincey hovering in the shadows of our stories this evening. Now it's time to stagger out and see what the night brings us.

Walking down Oxford Road, over the spectral battlefield of Peterloo, we come to the Town Hall, currently closed for renovations. In *Automated Alice*, Jeff Noon's 1988 reimagining of *Alice in Wonderland*, Alice tumbles down a rabbit hole, starting in the Victorian age and landing in a bizarre version of Manchester, circa 1998. She becomes entangled in a murder mystery, and races through the city in a search of clues. In particular, she spends a lot of time at the University and the Town Hall. Designed by Alfred Waterhouse, and completed in 1877, the Town Hall 'magnificently looms' over Albert Square in the centre of the city. The great hall was described by John Ruskin as 'the most truly magnificent Gothic apartment in Europe' (he never saw my student flat, clearly), and includes a series of twelve frescoes by the pre-Raphaelite artist Ford Maddox Brown, who has a Wetherspoon's named after him at the other end of Oxford Road.

In Noon's version, Alice is confused to see a memorial to Prince Albert, who had been very much alive when she went down the rabbithole, but is soon distracted by the strange creatures which inhabit Albert Square: 'people jigsawed together with objects, Pianogirls for example, and Soapboys, Curtaingirls and Wardrobing kids'. Inside, the

Town Hall is populated by the all-powerful Civil Serpents. The building is 'very echoey and very cold…a stonely warren of wanderings'. Alice thinks to herself that 'the strangest thing of all about the Town Hall was that they met absolutely no-one along their way. 'I always imagined that a Town Hall would be a very busy building,"' and her automated twin sister Celia replies 'Perhaps they do their business in secret'. Soon, though, they find a series of signs directing them to 'THE PRUNING DEPARTMENT, THE TREASURING DEPARTMENT, THE WHISPERING DEPARTMENT, THE TAXING DEPARTMENT and THE SLEAZING DEPARTMENT'.

Another short walk takes us to the Waterstones in Deansgate. The shop is the setting for a significant event in Sam Mills' 2012 novel *The Quiddity of Will Self*. The fifth section of the book is a loosely fictionalised account of the writing of *Quiddity* itself, narrated by a male 'Sam Mills'. This Sam Mills is down on his luck, and the section begins with him giving a reading in the branch, to 'three people clearly in need of medication'. The desolation and gnawing embarrassment of the failed event is acute: Mills is 'sat behind a lone desk, surrounded by unsold books. Twenty seven empty chairs give me cold metal stares'. Someone bumps into a display of 3-for-2 books in the history section, disturbing the author's flow: 'I want to set fire to the shop. I want them all to go up in flames'. The Q&A is even worse; one of the attendees goes on a diatribe about his own failure to get published, and an old woman asks Mills why he sets all his novels in Africa (she has mistaken Will Self and Wilbur Smith).

The event is redeemed only by the late arrival of a beautiful young woman who wants Sam to teach her creative writing. In the taxi back to his flat in Didsbury, Mills is more positive about the city: 'Manchester is my muse. Forget London and the Garrick; forget garrets in Paris; I've spent the last decade quaffing caffeine in Neros and Costas and other faux-Italian cafes that adopt a sunny piazza theme despite the northern rain that spits laughter at such an absurdity… tonight my eyes glaze the streets with an erotic psychogeography'. His reverie is only interrupted by the driver announcing that he too is a frustrated would-be author…

As Sam Mills left Waterstone's that evening, he may have passed two characters from *The Raw Shark Texts*, trying to break in. In Steven Hall's novel, Eric Sanderson, an amnesiac, is struggling to piece together fragments of his past, while trying to evade a conceptual shark, the Ludovician, which 'feeds on human memories and the intrinsic sense of self'. He is helped by Scout, who shows him a secret network of tunnels underneath Manchester, which can be accessed through the bookstore.

When they arrive in Deansgate, it is 'still dark, still very early. The city a quiet insomnia of smog, purple skies, puddles, rubbish and white and yellow sodium.' Sneaking into Waterstone's, they see 'bookshelves, the ground floor of the shop in night-time mode, still and silent with that half-strength 'we're closed' yellowy—orange lighting'. Heading for the 'H' section, they pull the books aside, unscrew a board, and find a 'three foot by four foot rectangular black hole', the entrance to a tunnel: 'I could see maybe two or three inches of grey bitty concrete floor before the space receded into complete black. The shop's dry warm processed air had made me start to sweat under my heavy coat but the air coming out of the hole felt cool and hard, basic and factual, and telling stories of miles of stripped-down empty places'.

After being pursued through the tunnels by the conceptual shark, they emerge in Central Library, where they search for shelter: 'stack by stack, stairwell by stairwell, we found our way into the deepest foundations of the library; a place of blinking old bulbs and shelf after shelf of turn-of-the-century books, sitting all dusty and quiet in their old-fashioned ranks.' Going further into the collection, they walk 'through the old towers of books and down an uncared-for staircase deeper into the stacks. Down here, the books were even older; sombre columns of washed-out grey and red leather covers curling away at the tops and bottoms of spines. They made me think of the old British army, the Empire army, abandoned and left behind, still standing in their dusty formations'. Finally, they reach the epicentre of the library: 'a great mound in the dim distant reaches of the stacks. A mound like the ones they buried ancient kings in, but a mound made from, instead of soil, all kinds of paper – newspapers, chip wrappers, glossy magazines, great strips of wallpaper, tiny labels and instruction manuals, heaps of plain and lined and letterheaded A4, the stripped-out leaves of diaries and ledgers and novels and photo books. Tons and tons of paper and all of it, every scrap covered, smothered, buried in lines and squares and triangles and swirls of blue and black and green and red biro words.'

Central library was opened in 1934 by George V. The folksinger Ewan MacColl remembered that 'the new Central Library which replaced the chicken house was an imposing circular structure with an enormous reading room, a small theatre and carrels where serious students could carry out their research without interruption. The portico of the magnificent edifice quickly became a popular rendezvous and "Meet you at the ref" became a familiar phrase on the lips of students, lovers and unemployed youths'. Later, Morrissey would try to hold a photoshoot in the Language and Literature section, but was thrown out by a librarian who didn't know who he was.

There have been a lot of changes to the library since Hall's novel was released – it was closed down in 2010, to repair the damage done by the Ludovician, with many of the rarer books stored in a Cheshire salt mine for safe-keeping. The grand reading room is now mainly used as a reference library, and the old language and literature section with its beautiful wooden shelving has been moved to the basement. The stacks where Eric and Scout sheltered stretch over four floors and include 35 miles of shelving, containing more than 1 million books.

Moving back up Oxford Road towards the Universities, we pass The Deaf Institute. The Grade II listed building was opened in 1878 for the benefit of 'deaf and dumb' (sic) inhabitants of Manchester.

A report from the time describes the facilities:

'The building includes one of the prettiest chapels arranged in ampitheatre form to be found outside a college, a large club and reading room, a smoking room and general offices; the basement is prepared for a gymnasium, but requires almost entire equipment.... A billiard table is about to be provided.' After years of neglect, the building reopened in 2008 as part of the Trof chain of bars and restaurants. Originally to be called 'Deaf and Dumb', mirroring the words carved above the door, the name was changed to The Deaf Institute for reasons of good taste. It has become a popular venue for live literature events, one of which was documented in Nicholas Royle's *First Novel* (2013).

Royle's protagonist, Paul Kinder, a creative writing lecturer struggling with the follow-up to his debut novel, is appearing at the second night of a new monthly event at the Institute. The event is organised by Chris Killen, not named in the book but described as 'a young writer who had just won a two-book deal with a fashionable publisher, but [who] was so modest and self-effacing in his skinny jeans and crumpled shirt, no one was anything but pleased for him. Plus he could write, which helped'. The first event had been held in the basement and proved 'unexpectedly popular… if you weren't standing by the bar, it was impossible to get a drink'. Now the event has moved to the upstairs room, which is 'much bigger with a proper stage, decent seating and a disco ball hanging from the high ceiling'.

Unfortunately, Kinder's reading doesn't go any better than Sam Mills'. As he finishes, and goes to retake his seat, another figure from the Manchester literary scene staggers towards him, and accuses him of having plagiarised *Fight Club*; then a friend queries the mechanics of a scene in which a character is decapitated by a low flying aeroplane. He leaves with his doubts about the work-in-slow-progress magnified.

Our literary meanderings are not be confined to the

Manchester

Oxford Road corridor. The Northern Quarter, a series of streets grouped around Oldham Street, just off Piccadilly Gardens, has been home to alternative Manchester for decades. In *Manchester, England*, his cultural history of the city, Dave Haslam quotes Charles Russell describing the street's already well-established nightlife in 1905: 'on Sunday evenings, there are three main points of attraction for working lads; Oldham Street, Market Street and Stockport Road. From Hulme, from Ardwick and from Ancoats they come in, in the main well-dressed, and frequently sporting a flower in the button-holes of their jackets'.

In *Cold Water*, her debut novel from 2002, Gwendoline Riley portrays the area's ubiquitous dive bars. Her protagonist, Carmel, works in one of these bars (which sounds like the Night and Day on Oldham Street), decorated 'in the American style... worn out red velveteen on the stools, the tables are battered dark wood and dusty artificial ferns froth in long brass planters between the booths'. The bar is peopled by hipsters like Kevin – in 'his own bubble... Bukowski, John Fante, all that hard-boiled stuff and mermaids and whisky and Japanese people being sick in each other's mouths'. She spends most of her shifts doing cryptic crosswords and reading Thomas Mann – the service in these places is never swift.

When she's not working, Carmel often finds herself drawn to Paramount Books, on the edge of the Northern Quarter, next to the Shudehill Interchange. A favourite of writers like Benjamin Myers, and perpetually threatening to close down, Paramount is open on Thursdays, Fridays and Saturdays, always smells of cooking, and, as Riley says, is marked outby the 'triumphal music blaring from the small speaker over the door and up the road' at all times. Slightly further along are the last surviving examples of the Book Exchanges, which sell 'videos, comics and porn mags. These are all in cellophane covers... If I see a man looking through them I'm always sure to stare and shake my head and hiss'. There are ghosts of these shops all over the Northern Quarter; faded window displays and burned out neon signs advertising 'BOOKS' above side street basements. Coincidentally, just around the corner from Paramount Books is the apartment where Will Self stayed to complete his novel *Shark*, an experience he wrote about in the New Statesman.

Riley also makes a passing reference to an idea for a short story called 'The Steepest Street in Manchester', which must be Jutland Street, close to Piccadilly station. Back in the *Life on Mars* days, police used to round up drunks in the back of a van, and then speed down the ludicrously steep cobbled road, before letting them out with a warning not to do it again.

The area around Canal Street has been associated with gay people since the Sixties, but it was the opening of Manto in 1990 which kickstarted the current club culture. As well as the bars, the Village also contains a statue of Alan Turing, and the only permanent memorial to people who have died, or have suffered from, HIV and AIDS. The most famous fictional depiction of the Village is Queer as Folk, but it does appear in literature too, notably Nicholas Blincoe's crime novel *Manchester Slingback* (1998). Blincoe's protagonist Jake Powell is a successful London businessman, but he is dogged by a police investigation which threatens to uncover secrets from his past as a hustler in the Village.

Returning to the city after more than a decade away, he returns to his old haunt via 'a network of alleyways… the streets were narrow, foreshortened by the Victorian warehouses that lined the way. The buildings could have been empty and derelict, they showed so few signs of life'. He cynically remarks that the regeneration of Manchester 'didn't extend as far as the backs of the buildings'. Emerging in the Village itself, he recognises The Thompson Arms (where I had a brief stint as a drag-act DJ), 'the dingy piano bar and nightclub set into the corner of the multi-storey, the same National Express coaches pulling round into Sackville Street. And, opposite the bus station, the same row of farmyard-style cottages, whitewashed in grey: a gay porn shop, a Chinese takeaway where the chip shop once stood'.

Later, he gets a potted history of the past 15 years from a regular at one of the longest-established bars: '1978, during that huge discotheque craze, we had a complete redecoration… 1985, I think, we laid a new carpet, which was a big thrill. Then, it must have been '93, the boards came off the windows… orders of the new management. I believe they wanted to let a little light in on the matter, but it was a horrible mistake. Most of us, we look our best at 30 watts and below'.

Ah, history, secrets and darkness. Circling back around towards the city centre, we find The Portico Library, its side door entrance rendering its visitors invisible to the regulars of the pub which now occupies the majority of its premises. The library is the scene of another literary event, portrayed in Emma Jane Unsworth's novel *Animals*, although this one goes off rather better than the previous two. Laura, a frustrated writer, is at the private library, built between 1802 - 1806, for a talk on Yeats. After climbing three flights of winding stairs (over the heads of the drinkers beneath), she finds 'the main room where the ceiling rose in a stained glass dome. It wasn't a large space, a square twenty meters, but it was airy and light, and had the vast tranquillity of libraries that's a lot like being outdoors; you feel like there's more air in those places'. Laura sees a few people milling around, and glances at a 'series of concertina'd screens pinned with what looked like charcoal drawings', but is more drawn to a table of red and white wine: 'free, and at lunchtime! I should really make an effort to come to more literary events'. She drifts through the talk on a cloud of wine and poetry; afterwards, she drinks two more bottles with the speaker, before rowing with her fiancée over the phone. Previous members of the library like Thomas de Quincey would surely have approved.

Emma Jane Unsworth called *Animals* 'a scamper around the city', and there are plenty of memorable descriptions of Manchester landmarks, particularly the 'monstrous blade-phallus of the Hilton Tower' and the vegan co-operative café in Hulme, populated by hippy types from the surrounding apartments, where Laura and her best friend Tyler go, sneaking their own ham and honey in to liven the food up (Tyler did ask if they served honey, once: 'they looked at me like I'd just slaughtered an orang-utan in front of them… and this was HONEY. It's a natural product. Bees LIKE MAKING IT. No one forces them to. Where will the madness end?')

Unsworth has always had a keen eye for unusual details about Manchester. In her debut, *Hungry, the Stars and Everything* (2011), she recounts a story about Satan appearing in the city centre: 'Back Pool Fold was a tiny street cutting between the buildings that made up the Town Hall annex. Legend had it that the devil had been sighted there back in 1863, in late December, when a crowd of horrified onlookers had watched, slack-jawed as – ever the cavalier spirit – he had casually walked along the sides of the buildings, branding the snow with coal-coloured hoofprints'.

Maybe that's where our walk should end. For all Manchester's ghosts, who can compete with Old Nick himself, sashaying along the walls of a building in full view? Manchester, where even the devil has to bring out his best moves if he wants to make a mark.

—Thom Cuell, Manchester (Summer, 2018)

Contributors

Thom Cuell is a founder and editorial director of *Dodo Ink*, and editor of *Minor Literature[s]*. His writing has appeared in *3:AM Magazine, Review 31* and elsewhere.

Tristan Burke was awarded his PhD in nineteenth-century literature from the University of Manchester in 2017. He has published essays and reviews on literature, cinema, philosophy and theatre in *Minor Lits*, *3:AM Magazine* and *The Manchester Review*. He is currently working on an academic study of nineteenth-century literature and literature.

Sian Cummins has MAs from Goldsmiths and Manchester and lives in Manchester with two cats and a small superhero. She has written for *Time Out* and *Creative Tourist*.

Peter Wild is the author of *The Passenger* and *Akira Kurosawa: A Critical Life*, and the editor of *The Flash, Perverted by Language, The Empty Page & Paint a Vulgar Picture*. He is also the proprietor of the *Bookmunch* blog.

Sarah-Clare Conlon, stints in Paris and London aside, has lived in the Rainy City since the halcyon Haçienda days. She is a freelance copywriter at *Manchester Confidential* and *Manchester Wire*, Literature Editor of *Creative Tourist* and a proofreader for Arts Council England and others. A Salt Prize winner for flash fiction and a Bath Flash Fiction Award longlistee, her work has also been published by Comma, *Pygmy Giant, Spelk, Stand and Flash: The International Short-Short Story Magazine*, who called her "one of the most interesting and inspiring authors writing flashes".

Anthony Trevelyan was born in 1973 and grew up in rural Lancashire. His first novel, *The Weightless World*, was published by Galley Beggar Press in 2015 and longlisted for The Desmond Elliott Prize in 2016. His second novel,

Claudia, was published by Sceptre in 2018. In addition to his writing Anthony frequently but no less awkwardly appears on stage, participating in such staples of the Manchester spoken-word scene as *FlimNite* and *First Draft*. He lived for many years in the Northern Quarter but more recently retreated to the suburbs and the slow death of home ownership.

Bryony Bates is a writer and performer based in Manchester. Her work has appeared in *Adjacent Pineapple* and *The Other Room Anthology*, and her debut solo pamphlet *States* was published in 2017 by Enjoy Your Homes Press. Her credits as a performer include *She Bangs The Drums, 15 Minutes* and *There is a Light: Brightlight* with Contact Young Company, as well as performance art events RITE and Creatures of Catharsis. Her work has been described as "examining complex political imperatives but pairing it with the fun and ridiculous" (MCR Live), "bleakly hard work" (Gloria Dawson, *Zarf*) and "flippant bullshit" (herself).

Valerie O'Riordan holds an MA and a PhD in Creative Writing from the University of Manchester. Her work has appeared in *Unthology, Tin House Online, LitMag, The Lonely Crowd, The Mechanics' Institute Review, Litro* and other journals. She is Senior Editor at *The Forge Literary Magazine*.

About Dostoyevsky Wannabe Cities

"We've gone on holiday by mistake"
Withnail & I

The anthologies in this series feature small selections of writing from particular cities (or areas of cities) around the world. Each book is a snapshot of writing from a particular time and space accompanied by a local event timed to coincide with publication. The series was conceived by Dostoyevsky Wannabe (based in Manchester, UK), works in association with Minor Literature[s] (London, UK) and in collaboration with an array of local independent literary groups.

The series was originally inspired by the array of independent DIY music scenes in the 1980s and 1990s in Olympia, Glasgow, Liverpool, Manchester, Coventry, Seattle, Dunedin and many others.

Book Cover Design

Dostoyevsky Wannabe co-founder Victoria Brown is the main art-director for this series.

**Forthcoming
on Dostoyevsky Wannabe Cities**

Norwich
Guest-Edited by Sophie Essex

Brooklyn
Guest-Edited by
Bill Lessard and Mary-Boo Anderson

Nottingham
Guest-edited by Miggy Angel

Glasgow
Guest-Edited by Laura Waddell

Coventry
Guest-Edited by Adam Steiner

Dundee
Guest-Edited by James Barrowman

Sheffield
Guest-Edited by Emma Bolland

Santiago
Guest-Edited by Jessica Sequeira

Madrid
Guest-Edited by Terry Craven & Paloma Reaño

More from Dostoyevsky Wannabe, 2018

DOSTOYEVSKY WANNABE ORIGINALS

Honest Days by Matt Bookin
The Peeler by Bertie Marshall
Lou Ham: RAS by Paul Hawkins
A Hypocritical Reader by Rosie Šnajdr
Dark Hour by Nadia de Vries
Yeezus in Furs by Shane Jesse Christmass

DOSTOYEVSKY WANNABE SAMPLERS

Cassette 85 Guest-Edited by Troy James Weaver

DOSTOYEVSKY WANNABE CITIES

Bristol Guest-Edited by Paul Hawkins

DOSTOYEVSKY WANNABE EXPERIMENTAL

Metempoiesis by Rose Knapp
Liberating the Canon Guest-Edited by Isabel Waidner
Sovereign Invalid by Alan Cunningham
Blooming Insanity by Chuck Harp
Girl at End by Richard Brammer

DOSTOYEVSKY WANNABE X

Poem, A Chapbook by Timmy Reed
The Rink by Aaron Kent

Dostoyevsky Wannabe

Printed in Great Britain
by Amazon